EX LIBRIS
PACE COLLEGE

41 PARK ROW, NEW YORK

DEVELOPMENT ADMINISTRATION
Concepts and Problems

DEVELOPMENT
ADMINISTRATION
Concepts and Problems

EDITED BY
IRVING SWERDLOW

1963

Syracuse University Press

Copyright © 1963
by Syracuse University Press
Syracuse, New York

ALL RIGHTS RESERVED

Library of Congress
Catalog Card: 63-19728

Manufactured in the
United States of America
by The Heffernan Press, Inc., Worcester, Mass.

HN
15.
595

Contents

CONTRIBUTORS vii

INTRODUCTION
>Irving Swerdlow ix

I. THE STRUCTURE OF DEVELOPMENT ADMINISTRATION
>Merle Fainsod 1

II. THE POLITICAL CONTEXT OF NATIONAL DEVELOPMENT
>Lucian W. Pye 25

III. GOVERNMENTAL ORGANIZATION AND METHODS
IN DEVELOPING COUNTRIES
>Jay B. Westcott 45

IV. CULTURAL HURDLES IN DEVELOPMENT
ADMINISTRATION
>Agehananda Bharati 68

V. MOTIVATION FOR CHANGE AND
DEVELOPMENT ADMINISTRATION
>Paul Meadows 85

VI. ECONOMICS AS PART OF DEVELOPMENT
ADMINISTRATION
>Irving Swerdlow 103

VII. PUBLIC ADMINISTRATION AND THE PRIVATE
SECTOR IN ECONOMIC DEVELOPMENT
>Everett E. Hagen 124

VIII. "PLANNING THE PLANNING" UNDER THE
ALLIANCE FOR PROGRESS
>Albert Waterston 141

Contributors

Dr. Merle Fainsod is Professor of Government and Director of the Russian Research Center at Harvard University where he has taught since 1933. In 1936 he was a member of the staff of the President's Commission on Administrative Management. He has served as Price Executive of Consumers Durable Goods in the Office of Price Administration, consultant to the Temporary National Economic Commission, and as Deputy Director of the Civil Affairs School at Harvard University. He is the author of such books as *International Socialism and the World War, How Russia is Ruled,* and *Smolensk Under Soviet Rule.*

Dr. Lucian W. Pye is Chairman of the Political Science section and Senior Staff Member of the Center for International Studies at the Massachusetts Institute of Technology. He has conducted extensive research in the countries of Southeast Asia, has been a consultant to various government agencies, and U.S. representative at international conferences. He is the author of *Guerrilla Communism in Malaya, Politics, Personality, and Nation Building,* is co-author of *The Politics of the Developing Areas* and *The Emerging Nations,* and is editor of the forthcoming *Communications and Political Development.*

Dr. Jay B. Westcott, Professor of Political Science at Syracuse University, served with the federal government in the Organization and Management Division of the Commodity Credit Corporation, the Foreign Service Planning Division, the Productivity and Technical Assistance Division of ECA and MSA, and as Deputy for Far Eastern Military Programs in the Office of the Assistant Secretary of Defense. He was a consultant to the government of Pakistan in the summer of 1960 and recently spent several months as Visiting Professor at the India Institute of Public Administration. He has written *Relations of Executive Agencies to the Office of the President* and *Translation of Logistics Programs into Procurement Requirements* for the Second Hoover Commission and an *Annotated Bibliography of Management Training for Public Service.*

Mr. Agehananda Bharati is Assistant Professor of Anthropology at Syracuse University. He has taught at the Orientalisches Institut of the University of Vienna, Delhi University, Banaras Hindu University, the Mahamukuta Buddhist University at Bankok, Tokyo and Kyoto Universities, and the University of Washington at Seattle. Mr. Bharati authored *The Ochre Robe* and numerous articles in the fields of sociology, anthropology, religion, and philosophy, and is a Contributing Editor to *Universitas* (Stuttgart), *Zeitschrift fuer Philosophische Forschung* (Meisenheim), *Philosophischer Literaturanzeiger* (Munich), *Philosophisches Lexikon* (Munich), and *Folia Humanistica* (Barcelona).

DR. PAUL MEADOWS 'is Chairman of the Department of Sociology and Anthropology at Syracuse University. He has taught at Northern Illinois University, Western Michigan University, Northwestern University, Montana State University, and the University of Nebraska. Dr. Meadows was formerly president of the Midwest Sociological Society and editor of the *Midwest Sociologist.* Dr. Meadows has co-authored *Social Problems and Social Policy* and *Selected Abstracts in Development Administration: Field Reports of Directed Social Change;* he has authored *Themes and Movements: Studies in Ideas and Social Action.*

DR. IRVING SWERDLOW is Professor of Economics and Chairman of the Faculty Committee for the Center for Overseas Operations and Research at the Maxwell Graduate School of Citizenship and Public Affairs, Syracuse University. Dr. Swerdlow has served with the federal government in the Works Projects Administration, the War Production Board, the Economic Cooperation Administration, and the Mutual Security Agency. He has been Deputy Controller and Chief of Division of Resources and Operating Reports of the United Nations Relief and Rehabilitation Administration, and an economic consultant to the Government of the Union of Burma. Professor Swerdlow gave editorial direction to ECA's *Recovery Guides* and with Harlan Cleveland edited *The Promise of World Tensions.*

DR. EVERETT E. HAGEN is Professor of Economics and Senior Staff Member of the Center for International Studies at the Massachusetts Institute of Technology. Dr. Hagen has served with the federal government as Director of the Division of Planning of the Office of War Mobilization and Reconstruction, in the Bureau of the Budget, and is presently consultant to various government agencies. He has written *The Economic Development of Burma,* and *On the Theory of Social Change,* and has contributed to *The Emerging Nations.*

MR. ALBERT WATERSTON is a member of the Development Advisory Service of the World Bank, where he is currently directing a study of the organization of economic planning in developing countries. Mr. Waterston has served in the federal government in the Foreign Economic Administration and in other capacities. He has had numerous IBRD missions, particularly to Latin America. Mr. Waterston is a co-author of *Economic Development of Mexico,* and has just recently authored *Planning in Yugoslavia* and *Planning in Morocco.*

Introduction

RECENTLY, the term "development administration" has become a fashionable expression. Its use seems to add a touch of sophistication to the more prosaic "public administration" and sets the user off as one of the *cognoscenti* who recognizes the important role of development in the current affairs of government. But, like so many colorful expressions, it is somewhat artificial. Its meaning is unexplored and deceptively vague, and it is in danger of becoming merely a slick expression for "good public administration" that adds nothing to professional vocabulary or to thinking about problems of public administration.

This is regrettable, because the concept of "development administration" as distinct from some other kinds of public administration is a useful one. There are, or should be, many important, clearly recognizable differences between public administration in a poor country striving to attain self-generated economic growth and public administration in high income countries. It is time to rescue the term development administration before it has lost its usefulness by becoming imbedded in general and differing usage. There is still time to give it a distinctive substance and set boundaries for its meaning that will keep it a useful as well as colorful expression.

To demonstrate the need and usefulness of the concept of development administration as a particular type of public administration, it is necessary to show that it involves special understandings required in underdeveloped countries. These must be perceptible at operating levels; that is, officials must make enough different decisions, adopt enough different policies, and engage in enough different activities to warrant the distinctive designation.

Perhaps the concept of development administration can best be conceived by comparing the tasks involved in administrating an urban renewal program and in operating a water department in an American city. Assume that both are equally well administered so that quality of performance does not make the difference. The water department has the job of maintaining an adequate

water supply and distribution system, planning for future requirements and expansion, reading meters and making appropriate
charges for usage, training employees, dealing with the public,
the budget director, the mayor, and the unions, purchasing and
maintaining supplies and equipment, and all the multifarious
activities of operating a program in a busy, changing city. Yet,
though broad and universal, these activities are significantly
different from those performed by the parts of city government
responsible for identifying the areas of the city to rebuild,
acquiring the resources and land, moving the people now living
in the area, redesigning the uses of area, contracting for rebuild-
ing and construction of the new buildings, and supervising the
construction and reintegration of the area into the life of the city.

Described functionally, the differences do not appear significant. Objectives and budgets must be established, employees
must be hired and trained, lines of authority established, and
progress evaluations prepared—all these are functions common
to any good system of public administration. Perhaps the difference lies in the degree of difficulty encountered in executing
these functions, the amount of "pioneering" required, and the
difficulties of finding adequate procedures for moving people
who are unwilling to move, for reconciling conflicting interests
in redesigning a section of the city, for establishing new relationships which involve major changes in how people and governmental agencies customarily do business.

Another, more direct way of stating the proposition that there
is a distinguishable and useful concept of development administration is to ask three related questions:

1. Is public administration in a high income country different
from that in a low income country?

2. If differences exist, are they significant or merely un-
important variations?

3. If there are significant variations, can they be related to
differences in patterns or systems of administration?

These are difficult questions, resting on the shaky assumption
of commonly acceptable meanings for such terms as "significant
differences" and "differences in patterns or systems of administration." There can be no quantitative measurement of significance and variation, only judgment based on subjective evalu-

ation of more or less unrepresentative experiences. Yet a line of reasoning can be developed that seems persuasive as at least a partial answer to these questions.

First, perhaps it can be shown that certain patterns characteristic of poor countries materially affect the nature of their public administration. These characteristics may exist in a much lower degree in high income countries.

Second, perhaps it can be shown that the role of government in poor countries attempting to achieve a satisfactory rate of economic development must be substantially different from the role of government in high income countries.

Third, perhaps it can be shown that the "structure" of government, on which so much of the economic and social change in poor countries depends, is different from that in high income countries.

Finally, the specific roles performed by public officials may be different in a poor country.

If the process of public administration could be reduced to a system of basic principles and doctrines and verbalized at levels of generality that describe actual administrative behavior, it might not be difficult to deduce special principles and doctrines from the above progression of "proofs." But of course no approach to administration could be more unrealistic. Public administration as a process of operations in human abilities and relationships can scarcely be reduced to any common principles except at relatively high levels of generality that are quite worthless for analytical or comparative purposes. Indeed, it is difficult to identify any usable "principles" of public administration except in terms of specific operating situations, a fortunate circumstance that saves the study of public administration from becoming only vague examination of selected moral precepts.

The essays in this book were designed for discussion at a faculty seminar of the Maxwell Graduate School of Citizenship and Public Affairs at Syracuse University. They were not planned to support a simple line of argument about the desirability of a concept of development administration. Rather, the authors were invited to discuss, within their special fields of competence, how the problems of public administration were being met in underdeveloped countries. Not all of the authors would agree that there is a useful concept of development administration, as distinct from public administration. What is lost in unanimity on this point is, I believe, more than fully compensated for by freshness of approach and broader based understanding of public administration in underdeveloped countries.

Professor Fainsod addresses himself to the structure of government in underdeveloped countries. He discusses the problems of public administration in these countries, problems that are nearly always more painful and numerous than in the advanced countries. In groping for useful answers to interminable problems, administrators attempt to accomplish by means of structure what seems impossible through more direct means—to improve the efficiency of public administration. The limitation of this emphasis on structure, as well as the need for improving the structure of administration, clearly applies with particular force to underdeveloped countries.

Professor Pye tackles the political context of public administration in new and developing countries. The extension of the nation-state structure to all areas requires the shaping of the political context underlying formal governments. The inadequacy of Western political theory in providing guidelines for building a nation state out of a traditional society is reflected in a blurring of the line between the bureaucratic and political facets of government. Without a strengthening of the representative political processes, it may be impossible to effect the necessary improvement of administration. Government and therefore public administration is significantly different in these new countries, desperately attempting to accelerate the modernization process.

The organization and management of governmental offices in underdeveloped countries have received very little specialized examination. Perhaps they would need little, if the management problems of both rich and poor countries were basically similar. Professor Westcott discusses these problems in his essay. The particular difficulties in management of public administration in poor countries demonstrate the intensity of the need for improved public administration.

In his essay on "Cultural Hurdles in Development Administration," Professor Bharati discusses traditional practices and attitudes which could retard or accelerate development operations. His study of the problems of conflict between tradition and change has relevance for those seeking to administer development in any country. Professor Bharati points out that success in gaining acceptance of modernization depends largely on the methods adopted rather than on the targets of development. Here the characteristics of the particular underdeveloped country or region clearly affect the functions of public administration.

One way of defining development administration is the "management of change." Professor Meadows feels that the clue to management of change lies in the meaningfulness of events to human beings, and we are urged to look into the frames of reference involved in human identifications and interpretations. The role of communication in these identifications and interpretations becomes particularly strategic in underdeveloped countries, and the public administrator must seek out strategies of communication which would motivate acceptance of change.

The most widely accepted element of development administration is its emphasis on economic growth. Here the mistaken identification (a) of modernization with economic growth, and (b) of economic growth with economic activity, only highlights the increased role that governments of poor countries must play in the modernization process. Public administrators are deeply, but not exclusively, involved in the problems of economic growth. Their understanding of economic concepts and relationships must be quite different than in more advanced countries. In my essay "Economics as Part of Development Administration," the attempt is made to show some of these understandings and some of the unique aspects of public administration in economic matters in poor countries.

An often neglected administrative corner in underdeveloped countries is the important relationship between public administration and the private sector. In his essay, Professor Hagen discusses the necessary contribution of both public and private sector to growth and the ways in which public administrators affect this growth. The underlying forces determining this relationship are examined as are the obstacles which hinder development of optimum relationships.

In the last essay in this book, Dr. Waterston analyzes a U.S. Government sponsored program, the Alliance for Progress, to show the role of planning in underdeveloped countries. His emphasis on the need for "planning the plan" points up a widespread characteristic of administration in underdeveloped countries—the attempt to plan superficially without due regard to resources and administrative capabilities and without recognizing that planning must be undertaken if modernization is to be accelerated.

Do these essays answer the questions posed earlier in this introduction? Regrettably they do not. They weren't designed to do so. I have no doubt that if they had been asked to do so the authors of these essays would have provided answers that would have been competent, scholarly, and contradictory.

But the essays do demonstrate that poor countries have special characteristics that tend to create a different role for government. These characteristics and this expanded or emphasized role of government, particularly as it affects economic growth, tend to make the operations of the public administrator significantly different. Where such differences exist, public administration can be usefully called development administration.

IRVING SWERDLOW

Syracuse, New York
Spring 1963

I

The Structure of Development Administration

MERLE FAINSOD

ANYONE who has traveled in underdeveloped countries and talked with those responsible for development programs soon runs into a familiar complaint. Over and over again he is told: "We know what needs doing; the real problem is how to get it done." Planners talk eloquently of goals and objectives, but administrative implementation tends to be neglected in favor of resounding policy directives which carry no executive bite.

Any realistic treatment of the structure of development administration must therefore begin with a caveat. At issue is more than the skeletal framework of organization for development. Blueprints and organization charts are meaningless fantasies unless manned by a corps of trained administrators equipped with the knowledge and resources to translate programs and policies into accomplishments and deeds. To function effectively, moreover, administrators must enjoy political support. They will be condemned to frustration if they are divorced from the underlying power structure of the developing nation. The most favorable setting for progress in development administration exists where a politically influential and dynamic modernizing elite strongly desires development and can successfully project this attitude into both the bureaucracy and the population at large.

To state the problem in this fashion is not to minimize the importance of governmental or administrative structure. It represents rather an effort to put structure into a meaningful context and to recognize that it is an instrument which cannot be separated from the objectives and capacities of those who use it. Structural arrangements, as ways of allocating authority and canalizing bureaucratic energies, will necessarily vary with the tasks to be performed. Changes or adaptations in structure emerge in response to new problems and pressures, bringing fresh priorities to the fore. Because significant structural changes

1

ordinarily involve redefinitions of organizational purpose as well as decisions about the locus of bureaucratic and political power, any drastic reorganization almost inevitably causes innovating forces to collide with traditional routines.

1

Development administration is a carrier of innovating values. As the term is commonly used, it embraces the array of new functions assumed by developing countries embarking on the path of modernization and industrialization. Development administration ordinarily involves the establishment of machinery for planning economic growth and mobilizing and allocating resources to expand national income. New administrative units, frequently called nation-building departments, are set up to foster industrial development, manage new state economic enterprises, raise agricultural output, develop natural resources, improve the transportation and communication network, reform the educational system, and achieve other developmental goals.

The innovating thrust of development administration and the magnitude of the administrative burden which it imposes can be illustrated from Indian experience. Under the aegis of the Indian Planning Commission, which was established in 1950, two Five Year Plans have been completed, and a third begun. Its scope is many-sided.[1] In the field of education, for example, India hopes by the end of the third Five Year Plan in 1966 to provide schooling for all children in the 8-11 age group, to double the number of people in the 11-14 age group (making schooling available to 30 per cent of the young people in this age range), and to provide education for a little more than 25 per cent of the 14-17 age group. At the university level, one of the primary aims is to raise the proportion of science students to 40 per cent, while substantially expanding technical education. Such plans require a vast and challenging expansion of teacher training programs and of laboratories, buildings, and other facilities.

The program for rural India contemplates a substantial increase in agricultural output and income to be achieved with the help of improved seeds and implements, larger allocations of fertilizers and pesticides, the introduction of soil conservation and land reclamation practices, irrigation projects, rural electrification, the promotion of village industries and credit, marketing, and processing cooperatives. The community development program is expected to cover the whole country by October 1963, and hopefully will draw villages into the planning effort by involving them more directly in the formulation and execution of agricultural programs.

Plans for industrial expansion rely heavily on the state sector. State enterprises are expected to bear the brunt of development in such diverse fields as steel, heavy engineering, machine-building, electric equipment, ship-building, chemicals, fertilizers, drugs and surgical instruments, cement, coal mining, oil refining, rail and air transport, and communication facilities. Plans for expansion of the private sector contemplate extensive state assistance and direction; thus the National Small Industries Corporation will undertake to aid and promote small enterprises engaged in the manufacture of bicycles, sewing machines, electric fans, builders' hardware, hand tools, and similar products.

India is committed to the creation of a socialist welfare state and the obligations assumed by government also embrace the expansion of public health services, housing, special provisions for the so-called backward classes, various forms of social insurance, employment exchanges, and other welfare schemes. Nor do these exhaust the responsibilities of India's development administrators. Central to the success of the plan is the problem of gathering the resources to support it—devising taxes, stimulating savings, encouraging foreign private investment, negotiating foreign assistance, promoting exports, limiting nondevelopmental imports, and administering foreign exchange and licensing controls.

This truly onerous array of functions, which in greater or lesser degree is assumed by many developing nations, would tax the administrative capacities of even the most highly developed countries. They understandably pose acute administrative problems for the developing countries. Typically, these nations start with great handicaps. Experienced administrators are scarce, and those who are available at the time when the development effort is launched have been trained with a narrow and restricted view of their functions. Few have the background or experience needed to shoulder the complex responsibilities which development tasks impose. Technical specialists are lacking in crucial fields, and domestic training facilities do not ordinarily exist. Expectations are high, while the capacity to fulfill them falls far short of urgent needs.

In countries which have only recently won independence, special complications attend the transition from colonial rule. The withdrawal of the imperial power is usually accompanied by a large-scale exodus of its experienced administrators, and the pressure to dispense with their services is frequently accentuated by nationalist fervor and the determination to "nativize" key administrative posts. At the same time the native administrators who served the imperial master tend to be distrusted by the freedom-fighters, who frequently install their own, often untrained, representatives, treating public office as a legitimate object of spoils. The morale and the efficiency of the civil service sharply deteriorate, precisely at the point when it is faced with new and ever-increasing demands.

A number of newly independent nations have sought to avoid these problems by building on their colonial past. Some, such as Pakistan and Nigeria, have gone to great lengths to retain expatriate administrators, at least for a transitional period during which replacements could be trained. In both India and Pakistan native administrators who had served the British were welcomed into the new services. They contributed significantly during the difficult partition period and provided an indispensable administrative base for launching more ambitious developmental efforts. British colonial tutelage, however distasteful to Indian freedom-fighters, helped ease the transition to independence by incorporating increasing numbers of native administrators in higher civil service posts, by providing increasing experience in self-rule, and by launching the rudiments of a development program in such fields as agriculture, irrigation, transportation, and education.

The degree of continuity visible in both India and Pakistan finds little reflection in many other ex-colonial areas. In Burma the mass expulsion of British and Indian civil servants after independence left the nation with only a handful of experienced senior Burmese administrators.[2] The elimination of the Dutch in Indonesia created an administrative vacuum into which freedom-fighters and lower-ranking clerical personnel flowed. In the even more extreme case of the Belgian Congo, indigenous representation in the colonial civil service was almost nonexistent, and virtually no preparations were made for the transfer of power.

Even in the administratively more advanced ex-colonial countries such as India and Pakistan, the heritages of the past interposed barriers to progress in development administration. The ICS (Indian Civil Service) cadres were able and experienced, but they were trained to stress the law-and-order and revenue-collection functions of the colonial period, and they found adjustment to a developmental perspective difficult. Members of an elite service which prized and rewarded the general administrator, they were slow to appreciate the special skills so essential to development, and they tended to ignore the specialists' claims for equal status and treatment. Elitism was also manifest in a tendency to perpetuate the tradition of aloofness, superiority, and paternalism which characterized the ICS under the British raj. Their conception of guardianship left little room for spontaneous, grassroots initiative and operated to keep the lesser breeds, inside and outside the administration, in their place.

In countries such as Iran, which were not subjected to the colonial experience, bureaucratic traditions were, if anything, more authoritarian and less oriented toward developmental goals. By and large, the bureaucracy existed to protect the interests of the leading land-holding families; the structure of administration and justice reflected this overriding concern. Modernization was primarily directed toward building military strength rather than reforming the social order; the bureaucracy operated as a conservative force to preserve the status quo. Administration tended to be family-intertwined, arbitrary, and particularistic in its incidence, and subject to purchase and sale. Such tradition-rooted bureaucracies are even less equipped to spearhead change than the ex-colonial bureaucracies.

2

What then are some of the characteristic administrative problems of developing countries? First and foremost, there is a general shortage of trained administrators with developmental skills, and a particular scarcity of men possessing technical knowledge and industrial and commercial experience. All too frequently, the few who have received adequate training or displayed outstanding administrative talent find themselves so overloaded with responsibilities that their effectiveness is dissipated. In the first stages of the effort to assemble and mobilize cadres, developing countries are perforce compelled to resort to a patchwork of makeshift arrangements. In India, for example, a special Recruitment Board was established in 1947 to conduct an emergency recruitment drive to fill vacancies left by the exodus of British and Muslim officers. Written examinations were temporarily suspended, and candidates in the twenty-seven to forty-five year range with five years of administrative experience were eligible for appointment in the Indian Administrative Service (IAS), successor to the ICS. The initial emergency recruitment of 1948-1950 was followed by another special recruitment drive in 1956-57, though this time written examinations were restored. The IAS was strengthened by drawing on the state services and the defense forces as well as by the "open market" special recruitment drives.[3]

In Pakistan, after partition, some twenty-six British ICS officers and five British members of the Indian Political Service were retained on contract, and emergency recruitments were conducted in 1952 and 1960.[4] On the other hand, no efforts were made to retain the British and Indian officers who dominated the Burmese service, and the yawning gaps at the senior level were filled by promotions from the suordinate services. In addition, the Burmese conducted examinations in which some members from the lower clerical grades qualified for promotion. In Indonesia vacancies were filled both by promotion and by the large-scale bestowal of office, frequently on unqualified freedom-fighters.

As these examples illustrate, the first generation of development administrators came from diverse sources, and their competence varied greatly. Few were prepared by training and experience for the novel developmental assignments which came their way. Most had to learn on the job, and while some responded magnificently to the challenge, there were many who were simply not equipped to cope with the large responsibilities which they assumed. Their own uncertainties and lack of confidence made them extra-sensitive to criticism, and defensive in responding to outside professional advice. In some instances, there was such a chasm between assigned tasks and the administrative capacity to fulfill them that failures in performance brought complete disenchantment with the very idea of development planning. Impatience for quick results led to profound disappointment when they were not forthcoming. In the cautious words of the 1961 *Report of the Burmese Public Services Enquiry Commission,*

> New and ever increasing demands of a democratic welfare state fell upon a civil service already seriously weakened by the exodus of many experienced officials at all levels. The new rulers . . . were enthusiastic, confident and infused with a sense of mission. Having led the country to Independence they desired to see their visions of the new Burma rapidly transformed into reality. The new rulers, like the civil servants, were . . . inadequately equipped for the gigantic task of rehabilitation, reconstruction, consolidation, and development. In their enthusiasm, they overlooked the fact that such colossal schemes as they had in mind took time to materialize . . .[5]

As more realistic perceptions of the requirements of development administration emerge, transitional improvisations tend to be supplemented by long-range personnel programs designed to produce administrative cadres better suited to developmental needs. Yet even the best of these programs runs into difficulties with the continuing pressure to politicize the public services and to use them for purposes which have little to do with developmental goals. Even in an administratively advanced developing country such as India where appointments to the higher services are largely based on merit and rigorous competitive examinations, one hears charges that family and political connections advance careers, that bribery and corruption are increasing, and that political pressure increasingly conditions administrative decision-making. Where traditions of administrative integrity and a merit civil service are less firmly entrenched or have never become established, the public services all too easily degenerate into a place hunter's paradise where followers of the dominant political leadership are rewarded with sinecures and opportunities for private profit.

The enormous increase in the size of the public services in many developing countries, while in part a legitimate response to new development activities, also functions as a partial substitute for a social security system for the favored needy. Since the average pay of government servants is low, they frequently treat supplicants for government favors as a legitimate source of additional income. At lower levels only small gratuities or gifts designed to facilitate access and speed consideration may be involved. At higher governmental levels the perquisites of office not infrequently become the springboard to private fortune and the enrichment of families and friends. In such circumstances, the distribution of the benefits of development administration are bound to be somewhat asymmetrical, and programs to improve the competence of development administrators are robbed of much of their intended effect.

Another recalcitrant sector in development administration is the difficult task of translating policies and plans into accomplishments and deeds. In most developing countries too little attention is devoted to what the Indian Planning Commission has described as "fixing specific individual responsibility for producing results within agreed time-schedules and in accordance with approved polities and programmes."[6] In part the problem is one of the attitudes of political leaders and responsible administrators, the fascination with large schemes, impatience with detail, and the absence of action-oriented plans. In part, difficulties are traceable to lack of qualified personnel at lower bureaucratic levels where responsibility for execution largely rests. There is a characteristically sharp falling off in the competence and training of administrators as one moves away from the center to the districts and localities where the direct impact of administration is felt.

At all levels execution tends to be hampered by a shortage of basic office skills—the absence of filing systems, the lack of trained stenographers, accountants, and office managers, and adherence to antiquated procedures which provide busywork for clerks but stand in the way of the expeditious disposition of public business. While these deficiencies are not easily remedied, more attention to these lower-level problems may well help break the bottlenecks which frustrate even the most promising development plans.

At a more basic level, programs generate resistance when their innovating thrust collides with traditions and customs to which people are deeply attached. In no area are these inbred resistances to change more stubbornly rooted than in the villages which still dominate the economies of most developing nations. They are reflected in the difficulties encountered in country after country in modernizing farm practices and raising agricultural output. They are registered in the disenchantment which has developed around community development programs, because the quick-working miracles which some expected have not occurred. The realization that modernization of agriculture in an underdeveloped country cannot occur overnight has come slowly. It is difficult enough to perfect the administrative procedure and techniques which will bring improved seeds, implements, fertilizer, and pesticides to the villages. But it is even more difficult to teach the villagers to use them and to persuade them to abandon the familiar practices for a completely untrod path. In such circumstances, the execution of development programs which depend on voluntary cooperation must inevitably be a slow and arduous process of explanation, demonstration, and persuasion; short cuts to utopia are not at hand.

3

The structural problems of development administration open up still another Pandora's box. Development usually involves the rapid multiplication of new administrative units, which have to be coordinated with each other and with existing departments as well. New functions tend to be given separate organizational expression. There is much to be said for such new organizations as path-breaking devices to liberate energies and emphasize priorities. Carried to an extreme, however, the proliferation of new organizations produces such a diffusion of power that the task of central direction and coordination becomes extremely difficult. Organizational problems which have plagued the most highly developed nations reappear in a not unfamiliar guise. Faced with the problem of coordination, most developed nations have grouped related functions in single departments or ministries, limiting the number of ministries to permit retention of direction and control by the top political leadership. The same pattern is visible in the developing countries, though there the problem is greatly complicated by the rapidity with which new functions emerge and the consequent structural fluidity.

In a number of new nations which were formerly under British control, the task of coordination has been eased by the cohesive force of a strong generalist administrative tradition. The tradition is institutionalized in an elite corps of general administrators who are usually recruited at an early age from the top stratum of university graduates and whose careers are deliberately designed to prepare them for increasingly broad and important coordinating responsibilities. In the Indian Administrative Service (IAS) and the Civil Service of Pakistan (CSP), for example, service as a district officer is usually followed by assignment to state and central secretariats. Officers are frequently rotated from job to job on the assumption that general administrative skills are readily transferable to a wide variety of substantive fields. Continuity in the secretariat at higher levels in India is ensured by the existence of a Central Administrative Pool of officers selected from the All-India and Class I Central and State Services, who are outside the rotation system and always available to the central government for high posts. At lower levels the Secretariat Service itself provides continuity. Specialists are relegated to departments in the ministries with departmental lines of responsibility running through the secretariat to the minister himself.

Since the members of the elite corps constitute a carefully selected and able group with a high degree of esprit de corps and since top positions in the secretariat are reserved for them, they in effect provide the framework within which administrative policy is coordinated and conflicts resolved. The unified discipline and direction which they supply constitute elements of administrative strength which can be fully appreciated only by examining the problem of administrative systems which give no weight to the generalist's role.

At the same time, the secretariat system has manifested certain weaknesses in coping with the increasing burden of new administrative responsibilities. One hears frequent complaints of delay, resulting from congestion of decision-making at the center and excessive centralization of power in the secretariats. An understandable distrust of the quality of lower level administration has led to this reluctance to delegate authority. One of the major impediments to quick action, however, can be traced to excessive layering in the secretariats themselves. After a file has worked its way through the various departmental levels, the customary procedure has required that it begin all over again at the lowest clerical level proceeding for notations through the various secretarial ranks up to the secretary's desk. Procedural slavishness and dilatory tactics at lower levels have created bottlenecks which only heroic action can break.

In an effort to accelerate secretariat business both India and Pakistan have introduced so-called section officer schemes which remove subordinate clerical personnel from the line of decision and route papers for substantive action to a responsible undersecretary or assistant secretary. Files are also classified according to importance so that many matters can be settled short of reference to the secretary himself. Nehru's Statement on Administrative Procedure laid before Parliament on August 10, 1961, goes even farther and calls for the delegation of greater powers to ministerial departments, their liberation from itemized financial controls in the post-budget period "except on vital matters," and the decentralization of Planning Commission controls.[7]

In some instances even more drastic reforms are contemplated. The 1960 *Report of the Andhra Pradish Administrative Reforms Committee* called for a merger of the offices of the heads of department with the secretariat as the "only practical solution" to the problems of shared and duplicated administrative responsibility.[8] The 1961 *Report of the Burmese Public Services Enquiry Commission* also recommended the formation of "integrated" ministries, though it cautiously suggested integration "in one or two Ministries as a pilot scheme" prior to any government-wide changes.[9]

The strength of the administrative generalist tradition in developing nations such as India and Pakistan has its obverse side in a certain tendency to look down upon specialists. The persisting notion of elite service is visible in more favorable pay scales, jealously guarded powers, and higher prestige. At the same time the complex tasks of development and industrialization call for more specialized knowledge and technical skill. Virtually all developing nations have a crying need for engineers, scientists, doctors, technicians, industrial managers, and agricultural specialists. Since many of these nations place heavy reliance on the public sector to spearhead development, they must create attractive conditions of public employment for the sorely needed specialists.

The problem of generalist versus specialist and the task of regulating their interrelationships raise issues of the gravest difficulty in developed as well as underdeveloped countries. But these issues take different form in the two instances. While the more developed countries are relatively well-supplied with specialists and must prevent professionalism from running rampant, the less developed nations must build up and train corps of specialists on the basis of which development can take place. The specialist must be given an honored place in administration, sharing the perquisites, the prestige, and the responsibilities which were formerly reserved exclusively for the elite administrative service. The all-purpose general administrator must probably become something of a specialist himself. In India, for example, a certain proportion of the elite service has already been reserved for secretarial service in specialized fields, and rotation in assignments has been limited by requiring officials "in key posts" to remain in their jobs for at least five years.[10] It would, of course, be unfortunate if specialization jeopardized the vital contributions of general administrators. The danger, though occasionally feared, appears remote. As H. M. Patel, an ICS veteran, recently noted:

> There is a tendency to extol the merits and the value to the country of the technologists, the engineers and the scientists, and simultaneously to run down the administrators. There can be no objection to singing praises of the former. But it is unnecessary to institute a comparison and to say that one is more valuable than another. Each has a role to perform, and each would be handicapped without the other.[11]

Patel rightly stresses the collaborative ideal which should bind generalist and specialist, though he perhaps fails to emphasize that a relationship, which has historically favored the generalist, stands badly in need of balance.

4

Another major structural problem of development administration concerns the role of the planning organization in the governmental and administrative process. The range of issues involved can be suggested by a series of questions. Should the planning organization be established as an advisory body or as an agency with powers? Where should it be located in the governmental structure in order to function with maximum effectiveness? How should it be staffed and organized in order to facilitate the preparation of a coherent development plan? How can it be coordinated with administrative machinery in order to tap departmental expertise, minimize conflict, and ensure the implementation of approved projects and programs? How can popular planning and support for the program be organized most effectively? Needless to say, no single organizational pattern can be suggested which will be applicable or acceptable to all developing countries. Such factors as the nature of the economy, the existing political and administrative structure, the goals and scope of development, and the roles assigned to the public and private sectors may dictate quite diverse arrangements.

Experimentation with planning bodies has thus far run a broad gamut. In some countries all planning responsibilities are concentrated in a cabinet ministry of planning; in others planning units have been established in ministries of finance or economic affairs. In still others an independent planning commission has been established, sometimes, as in Pakistan, located in and responsible to the office of the president. In others the commission constitutes a cabinet committee composed of the ministers responsible for economic affairs.

India utilizes an ingenious combination in which the Prime Minister serves as chairman of the Commission, the Minister for Planning who is also responsible for liaison with Parliament acts as deputy chairman, while the remaining membership consists of the ministers for finance and defense, four members with ministerial rank who devote themselves exclusively to the affairs of the Planning Commission, and the Honorary Statistical Adviser to the Government who serves as a de facto member.

The Secretary to the Cabinet is also, ex officio, the Secretary to the Planning Commission. In Indonesia, the National Development Council, which drafted the 1960 Eight Year Plan, consists of no less than seventy-four members chosen by President Sukarno, with the chairman of the Council serving as an ex officio member of the Cabinet.

Some of these arrangements appear to hold out greater promise than others. As might have been expected, the Indonesian Eight Year Plan emerged as a miscellany of largely uncoordinated projects.[12] Experience thus far also suggests that locating over-all planning units in a ministry which is on a par with other ministries greatly complicates the task of coordination. Depositing planning powers in a ministry of finance offers the advantage of coordinating project and budgetary planning, but risks subordinating developmental objectives to narrow fiscal considerations. On the other hand, free-floating planning agencies remote from the seat of political power and armed with no mandate except to prepare a development plan are usually doomed to ineffectiveness.

A planning agency needs the enthusiastic support of the dominant political leadership. While such support provides no guaranty, it is an essential prerequisite of success. For this reason, it is ordinarily desirable to locate the planning agency at a point in the administrative structure where it has ready access to high level political leadership and, wherever possible, to have the prime minister or leader of the government serve as responsible head of the planning body. The Indian scheme, for example, squarely associates Nehru's power and prestige with the work of the planning commission. Although nominally an advisory body, the Indian Planning Commission, in effect, functions as a super-coordinating agency in the developmental area.

The staffing of planning agencies presents a difficult problem in most developing countries. Highly trained native economists, engineers, and other technical specialists are at a premium, and the basic statistical data so essential to planning are either non-existent or at best fragmentary. In many cases, foreign advisers have been utilized to compensate for the absence of local skills, but the results have varied greatly depending on the degree of local receptivity to outside counsel, the quality of the advisory staffs, and the extent of their involvement in the local scene. Even where central planning agencies have qualified personnel in key positions, there is usually a notable falling off of planning expertise in the ministries and departments and at regional and local levels. Typically, the schemes originated at the local level or in the ministries are poorly prepared and inadequately worked out. The major burden of transforming them into workable projects and relating them to each other falls on a small key group in the central planning body. These central planners frequently are deeply resented by those whose projects they have reworked and accused of practicing over-centralization and stifling local initiative. Ideally, there should be competent planning units in the ministries and in the localities, but so long as trained planners remain scarce, their most effective utilization and distribution will continue to present a troublesome challenge.

Coordination of planning and administration is vital to a successful development effort. It is particularly important that the planning agency maintain close liaison with the ministry of finance to ensure that the annual budget and the development plan march in step. In India, as was noted earlier, the Minister of Finance is a member of the planning commission; without some such arrangement for budget coordination, a country's Plan may well turn out to be meaningless. The effectiveness of the Plan, moreover, hinges on the existence of machinery for its implementation. The Plan must be translated into specific targets for each administrative sector, time tables and work schedules must be fixed, responsibility for program execution established, and performance regularly tested and checked. Unless the planning agency is able to project this type of control into administration, it risks spinning visions in a vacuum. Planning and administration cannot be compartmentalized without injury to both.

Nor can planning agencies succeed without popular understanding and consent. In many of the developing nations high illiteracy rates, poorly developed communication media, the isolation of the villages, and traditional attachments interpose formidable obstacles to innovation in any form. It is not uncommon in developing countries to discover that many villagers have not even heard that their nations have a Plan. Measures such as Pakistan's Basic Democracy Ordinance and India's experiment in democratic decentralization represent interesting efforts to involve villagers in grassroots planning, even though on a limited scale. The community development programs which have been launched in many of the developing nations rely heavily on village-level workers to link the national development program and village aspirations and needs. While these measures must naturally be slow-working, they constitute promising beginnings in creating understanding and a sense of popular participation in the planning process. Planning bodies cannot manufacture consent; they must in the ultimate analysis rely on political leadership and a supporting administrative apparatus to mobilize the popular energies which give life to their plans.

5

The management and control of the public enterprises which have proliferated in many developing countries pose another major problem. Whether trading companies, industrial undertakings, or credit institutions, these enterprises call for a variety of skills rarely found in the bureaucracies of developing nations. Efficient management of public enterprises demands a flexibility of action ordinarily inhibited by established governmental procedures and routines.

Most developing nations have acknowledged these compelling necessities by establishing their public enterprises as government corporations which, in theory at least, possess a degree of autonomy uncommon for ordinary government departments. But, in practice, many government corporations in developing countries remain subject to the usual range of personnel and fiscal controls. Often after freedom has been accorded, dramatic instances of corporate mismanagement have quickly brought new restrictions which seriously limit the corporate enterprises' autonomy. Form therefore should not be confused with essence. Not every government corporation, labeled as such, enjoys the freedom of action which is one of its claimed virtues.

Most government corporations in developing nations suffer from a shortage of top management, entrepreneurial, and technical skills. In a study of Burmese public enterprise, Khin Maung Lwin, the senior executive officer of the Pyinmana Sugar Mill in

Burma, writes: "The topmost problem and the one for which [a] solution has not yet been found is the lack of experienced executives to manage the newly established industries of the state."[13] Dr. Mohammed Sadli of the University of Indonesia in a parallel study of Indonesian public enterprise concludes that "the most important factor" in explaining the low efficiency of state enterprises is "the lack of skill, administrative, technical, and managerial."[14] Similar complaints have been voiced in Pakistan, India, and many other developing countries.

Efforts to cope with the problem have combined large doses of improvisation with long-term plans to prepare trained cadres. M. Ayub, the former director of the Pakistan Industrial Development Corporation, noted in 1959:

> Large-scale use of civil servants in state industrial enterprises is often not a matter of choice but of necessity. Experienced industrial and business managers and accountants are simply not available. Some stopgap arrangements have, therefore, to be made if under-developed and backward countries are to embark on the industrial road.[15]

The appointment of civil servants to top managerial positions in public enterprises has not always been an unqualified success. Some have made admirable records. But many senior civil servants have encountered great difficulty in readjusting to an entrepreneurial outlook and mastering the unfamiliar problems of costing, inventory control, manufacturing schedules and standards, investment and price decisions, and labor-management relations associated with the direction of public enterprise. What Khin Maung Lwin says of Burma has wider application:

> Since the Government is hard put to find trained top executives to manage a new State industrial concern a senior civil service official is usually appointed as a General Manager or the Chief Executive Officer to head the industry about which he has no previous first-hand knowledge. In many cases a retired civil servant has been selected to head the new industry. The art of management of an industrial enterprise has been learnt through the trial and error method and by the time some knowledge is gained about management, the official is either forced to leave

the job for reasons of health or he just becomes tired of struggling hard in the midst of problems pressing for immediate decision and goes back to his civil service post.[16]

In some instances, the managerial birth pangs associated with the burgeoning of public enterprises have been eased by the employment of foreign management consultants and technicians, but native pride and sensitivities have usually barred the transfer of substantial responsibility to foreigners and thus limited the effectiveness of their contribution.

At the same time promising steps have been taken to supply trained and experienced managerial and technical personnel over the long term. Both India and Pakistan have established industrial management pools specifically to meet the staff needs of state enterprises. Ambitious programs have been launched to train needed cadres both abroad and at home. Many students as well as more senior personnel have been sent abroad to attend schools of business administration and engineering colleges and to work in plants where they can obtain the needed experience. On-the-job training schemes in state enterprises and short-term management training programs are being supplemented with new schools of industrial management and engineering, designed to meet the long-term demand for skilled managerial and technical personnel in both public and private sectors.

Until these training programs begin to make a substantial impact, the management of public enterprises will present serious problems. Indeed, some developing countries increasingly realize that the rapid expansion of the public sector has overstrained available administrative resources. In Burma, for example, there is presently little disposition to launch new state enterprises. The Pakistan Industrial Development Corporation (PIDC) associates private capital in its ventures and sells its completed projects to private entrepreneurs "whenever the time is opportune and a reasonable price is forthcoming." M. Ayub, the former chairman of the PIDC, has ventured the judgment "that while the PIDC enjoyed an advantage over private parties in planning and erecting factories, it was at a disadvantage in the operation of the factories built."[17]

The low operational efficiency of many public enterprises and occasional dramatic revelations of corruption and mismanagement have led to severe restrictions on autonomy. In many developing countries public corporations are subjected to detailed government control of their personnel, investment, and price policies, as well as their financial expenditures, while pay scales and service conditions are assimilated to those of the regular government departments. Accountability to parliamentary bodies, where they exist, does not differ significantly from the normal ministerial pattern. While the failure to make effective use of the corporate form registers the strength of traditional control procedures as well as the distrust generated by poor performance, it also reflects an inadequate appreciation of the potentialities of the public corporation as a mode of conducting public business. Often the best public enterprises are caught in a vicious circle. Where good managers exist, they are frustrated by their lack of authority. Failure to delegate power in turn denies managers the chance to show their ability.

As more trained and experienced personnel become available to the public corporations, there will probably be a greater disposition to increase their freedom of action. Indeed, there are already signs in some of the administratively more advanced developing countries such as India of a determination to accord greater autonomy to the public corporations. The Indian third Five Year Plan recommends that "Secretaries to the Ministries should not be appointed as Chairman or Directors," though it adds that it may "be useful, in the initial stages, to appoint one or two directors from amongst government officials who are actually dealing with the project in the administrative Ministry concerned and in the Finance Ministry."[18] Boards of directors and general managers of corporations are to be given greater powers. The general manager, for example, can overrule his financial adviser's objections to specific transactions which have been approved by the Board of Directors. Parliamentary accountability is to be enforced through a special Committee of Parliament for State Undertakings, which will replace the present double gauntlet of detailed inquiry by the Estimates and Public Accounts Committees. Whether the new committee will do a better job than its predecessors remains to be seen. Much will depend on how it conceives its task. The temptation will always be great to concentrate energies on hunting out and publicizing individual mistakes rather than appraising the over-all efficiency and performance of the enterprises. As Ambassador Galbraith recently put it in an address before the Indian Society of Public Administration, "Autonomy does not mean less public accountability. If anything it means more—but it is accountability not for method, procedure or individual action but for result."[19]

6

The remaining consideration is the question of how the training of public administrators can be more effectively adapted to the needs of development administration. Shortages of crucial skills in developing nations give particular urgency to issues of manpower planning, educational reform, and training programs for the public service. Awareness of anomalies is not lacking, though prescriptions to deal with them are more difficult to effect. Pitamber Pant, the head of the Perspective Planning Unit in the Indian Planning Commission, recently wrote:

There has been substantial expansion of higher education in India in recent years and enrollment has been increasing at the rate of almost 9 to 19 per cent a year. In the absence of adequate avenues for technical and professional training or of employment on the completion of the secondary education, a very large proportion of students who pass the final examination seek admission to universities and colleges. Many of them are ill-equipped for higher education, but persistent demand for unrestricted admission to universities in arts and commerce courses continues. Often the graduates turned out can do nothing better than clerical work and even for this the avenues for employment do not expand in proportion to the number of graduates turned out. There is a great deal of waste involved in this attitude of drift. . . . When the need is for more engineers, scientists, and doctors, there is really no point in continuing to turn out graduates in arts, commerce, law, etc. in very large numbers, far too many in fact to have any reasonable chance of fitting into the developing pattern of the economy. . . . The limited resources should be directed to strengthening scientific, technical and medical education, improving laboratory and library facilities, and expanding scholarship schemes as much as possible, so that we get able engineers, doctors, scientists, research workers, and teachers in adequate numbers and of high quality, as these are the people whom we shall so badly need, and on whom the progress of the country will largely depend.[20]

As Pant indicates, the educational system of India, and indeed of most developing nations, is not presently well adapted to provide the array of special skills which industrializing and modernizing goals impose. But along with building up technical competence, there is the fundamental need to eradicate illiteracy, to inculcate nation-building values, and to supply elementary job training geared to the development plan. At every stage of education there is the problem of raising standards of academic excellence in the face of overcrowded facilities, overburdened teachers, and inadequately prepared students. Above all an analytical and problem-solving approach to learning must displace the habits of memorization and rote learning which reinforce the *bābū* mentality with its inflexible attachment to outmoded precedents and procedures.

Public service training programs in most developing nations face the special challenge of overcoming the disabilities of the educational systems on which they are superimposed. In recent years, public service training institutions have mushroomed in every corner of the developing world, and many civil servants from these areas have been sent for special training to the more developed nations. While the total impact of this effort is no doubt beneficial, the content and quality of instruction vary greatly, and emphasis on economic and political development is not always given its deserved importance.

Indian arrangements for public service training to meet the administrative needs of a developing economy stand out as particularly impressive. The National Academy of Administration at Mussoorie is a major center for various training programs. Its activities include: (1) a five-month combined course for recruits or probationers to the All-India and Class I Central Services. This innovation is designed to break down the exclusivism of the separate services and to build a servicewide esprit de corps,

(2) an additional seven-month course for IAS recruits, (3) a two-month course for older members of the IAS who entered the service under the Emergency Recruitment scheme, and (4) a six-week refresher course for IAS officers with ten to fifteen years of experience and for senior officers of other services.

The curriculum for probationers has been drastically revised in recent years to stress a development orientation. While IAS recruits are still taught to ride and shoot in the old British district tradition, they and their probationer colleagues must study economics, the five year plans, the Constitution of India, and public administration, and also attend lectures by development administrators, and visit various development projects. Perhaps even more important, they are encouraged to think for themselves and the problem-solving approach is built into the curriculum by requiring groups of students, known as syndicates, to address themselves to urgent administrative issues. Even more stress on syndicate work is incorporated in the special training program for senior officers.

In addition to the National Academy at Mussoorie, there are special schools for probationers in the Revenue, Audits and Accounts, Police, and Railway Services. The Ministry of Community Development and Cooperation presides over a complex network of training institutions extending from village-level workers up to the Central Institute of Study and Research in Community Development at Mussoorie which brings together development commissioners, collectors, senior district planning officials, block development officers, etc., to think through solutions to practical community development problems.

At a very different level there is the Secretariat Training School in New Delhi, which provides courses for Section Officers, Assistants, and Lower Division Clerks, teaches typewriting, and administers tests in stenography. Its curriculum, incidentally, includes lectures on planning and economic development. In addition, there is the Administrative Staff College at Hyerabad, which brings representatives of the private and public sectors together in a course of study closely patterned on the model of the British Staff College at Henley. Under the imaginative leadership of Professor V. K. N. Menon, the Indian Institute of Public Administration with its affiliated School of Public Administration, its journal, its publications, its branches, and its projected case program, has given a significant impetus to the professionalization of the Indian public services and stimulated a growing awareness of emerging problems in the development field. Finally, mention should be made of the many interesting training programs in the states, including those which have been recently set up in Rajasthan, Bihar, and Uttar Pradesh to prepare recruits for services connected mainly with district administration.

Yet, impressive as the Indian effort has been, it too is vulnerable to criticism. Admirable progress has been made, on the whole, in sensitizing the general administrator to his new developmental responsibilities. Less attention has been devoted to training engineers and scientists, professional economists, and managers of public enterprise. While plans to remedy these deficiencies will, no doubt, eventually be effective, the interim prospect is one of continuing difficulties and strain in meeting technical and scientific needs.

Improvements in the effectiveness of development administration ultimately depend on the quality and training of the public servants who man it and on a social and political environment which liberates their energies. Structural adjustments can work no developmental miracles where administrative manpower is inadequate or the will to develop is lacking. The secret of development is not concealed in the interstices of governmental or administrative structure. Development takes place where skill is supported by commitment and the human material resources exist to translate dreams into actualities.

NOTES

1. Planning Commission, Government of India, *Third Five Year Plan*, 1961.

2. "Out of the top 50 . . . , 33, two-thirds had gone; and of the top 25 only 4 remained. In the Police service, so essential for the maintenance of order, out of 37 officers with the rank of District Superintendent or higher, 31 had gone." J. S. Furnivall, *The Governance of Modern Burma* (New York: International Secretariat, Institute of Pacific Relations, 1958), p. 28.

3. "Of the 1,830 officers in position in 1962, 216 were drawn from the

old Indian Civil Service; 91 from the Defense Forces against vacancies renewed for war services officers; 198 from the 'open market' by two special recruitments in 1956-57; 598 by way of direct recruitment on the results of competitive examinations held from 1948 onwards until 1960; and 727 from State Services appointed either by selection or promotion." T. X. A. Srinivasavaradan, "Some Aspects of the Indian Administrative Service," *The Indian Journal of Public Administration*, VII, No. 1 (January-March, 1961), 26.

4.   Ralph Braibanti, "The Public Bureaucracy and Judiciary of Pakistan in Transition," paper prepared for the Conference on Bureaucracy and Political Development, sponsored by the SSRC Committee on Comparative Politics, held at Stanford, California, January 29-February 2, 1962, p. 8.

5.   Government of the Union of Burma, 1961, pp. 1-2.

6.   Planning Commission, Government of India, *Third Five Year Plan—A Draft Outline*, 1960, p. 59.

7.   For the text, see *The Indian Journal of Public Administration*, VII, No. 3 (July-September, 1961), 264-70.

8.   For summary, see *The Indian Journal of Public Administration*, VII, No. 1 (January-March, 1961), 101-6.

9.   *Ibid.*, pp. 133-35.

10.   Statement on Administration Procedure laid before Parliament by the Prime Minister on August 10, 1961, *The Indian Journal of Public Administration*, VII, No. 3 (July-September, 1961), 266.

11.   *Ibid.*, H. M. Patel, "Efficiency and Economy—Review of Past Experience," pp. 238-39.

12.   Guy J. Pauker, "Indonesia's Eight Year Development Plan," *Pacific Affairs*, XXXIV, No. 2 (Summer, 1961), 115-30.

13.   Khin Maung Lwin, "Development of Public Industrial Enterprises in Burma," paper prepared for the Seminar on Management of Public Industrial Enterprises, sponsored by the Government of India and the United Nations, New Delhi, December 1-11, 1959, p. 8.

14.   *Ibid.*, Mohammed Sadli, "Structural and Operational Aspects of Public (Especially Industrial) Enterprises in Indonesia," p. 21.

15.   *Ibid.*, M. Ayub, "Some Aspects of Management of Public Industrial Enterprises in the ECAFE Region," p. 6.

16.   *Op. cit.*, p. 9.

17.   *Ibid.*, M. Ayub, "Public Industrial Enterprises in Pakistan," p. 11.

18.   Planning Commission, Government of India, *The Third Five Year Plan*, 1961, p. 268.

19.   J. K. Galbraith, "Public Administration and the Public Corporation," *The Indian Journal of Public Administration*, VII, No. 4 (October-December, 1961), 466.

20.   Pitamber Pant, "Manpower Planning and Education," *The Indian Journal of Public Administration*, VII, No. 3 (July-September, 1961), 329.

II

The Political Context of National Development

LUCIAN W. PYE

1

FOR THE past three hundred years a constant theme recurring throughout the apparently haphazard process of Western contacts with the rest of the world has been the stubborn and ceaseless efforts of the European state system to transform all societies into replicas of the nation state. To the European mind it was inconceivable that anyone not be governed by an impersonal state and not feel a part of a nation. The European system required all territory to fall under some specific jurisdiction, every person to belong to some polity, and all polities to behave as proper states within the family of nations.

Wherever Europeans have gone they have generally displayed their impatience with any other arrangement of social life and devoted their surplus of energy and resources to the end of bringing others in line with the standards of the modern nation state. Throughout this period men who felt a responsibility for maintaining the stability and the easy working of the nation-state system regarded as a fundamental threat all domestic forms of authority which failed to meet minimum standards of nation statehood. This concern has left its mark on the European mind. It is reflected in the intolerance of Westerners toward all who fail to meet these minimum standards—a feeling which is at the same time disturbing to Westerners, acutely conscious as they are of the evils of ethnocentrism. It is also reflected in the Western insistence that societies which do not voluntarily act as nation states must be compelled to do so, even if this means direct assistance and open intervention in their affairs.

This is one way of looking at the long history of Western dealings with the rest of the world. From such a view there is a thread of continuity from the first early efforts of the British and Dutch, the French and the Americans, to persuade the traditional

25

rulers of India and China, of Java and the rest of Asia to adhere to Western notions of international law and usage. When the indirect approach proved inadequate, there came the phase of colonialism during which representatives of the nation-state system imposed upon recalcitrant traditional societies the infrastructure of the nation state in the form of Westernized administrative structures. And now that colonialism is ended, we see the United States and others through various forms of foreign aid and technical assistance continuing the effort to shape numerous, loosely structured societies into reasonable facsimiles of the modern nation state.

It is now evident that we are engaged in a long historical process involving two, not always harmonious, levels of change. The first level of change we can call modernization. This is the process of profound social change in which tradition-bound villages or tribal-based societies are compelled to react to the pressures and demands of the modern, industrialized, and urban-centered world. This process might also be called Westernization, or simply advancement and progress; it might, however, be more accurately termed the diffusion of a world culture—a world culture based on advanced technology and the spirit of science, on a rational view of life, a secular approach to social relations, a feeling for justice in public affairs, and, above all else, on the acceptance in the political realm of the belief that the prime unit of the polity should be the nation state.

At another level is the historical development of a system of international relations in which the nation state is again the prime unit. The development and maintenance of the nation-state system has been instrumental in diffusing the elements of modernization throughout the world; and in turn the modernizing process, by creating tensions and instabilities in formerly static societies, has created disruptive forces which threaten the stability of the entire international system of nation states.

Thus those who feel a sense of responsibility for maintaining international stability are striving to facilitate the process of modernization so that all societies can become stable states while at the same time seeking to prevent this very process of social change from disrupting the stability of the international system.

The resulting struggle explains the prime purposes of American foreign policy efforts in this era.

Before turning to the present scene it is well to make another historical observation. We have noted that the continuous process of extending the nation-state system to all societies has involved three stages: (1) initial efforts to persuade traditional authorities to adhere to international standards, (2) colonial administration and foreign rule, and finally (3) indirect assistance and foreign aid. These three stages very roughly coincide with three others which reflect the different aspects of government which at different times were thought to be the most important in giving a society the critical qualities of a modern nation state. These stages also represent the progressively deeper involvement of representatives of the international system in the domestic modernization process in transitional societies. Such involvement progressed from a concern with the formal, surface qualities of the nation state to an appreciation of the more fundamental political dynamics underlying the structure of the state.

During the first stage Europeans were uneasy about encountering societies which did not possess what they had come to accept as the kind of legal system essential to a modern nation. Not only did they find intolerable the lack of standardized rules and regulations based upon universalistic considerations, they also became convinced that the ultimate test of nationhood, and of membership in the community of modern states, depended upon the introduction of a Europeanized legal system. Thus the initial concept of political development focused upon the establishment of legal institutions. The introduction of extraterritoriality as demanded by the European powers in Turkey, China, Japan, and other countries of the non-Western world testifies to this preoccupation with legal institutions in building a modern state. In a very few cases the pressure of the international system for legal reforms was adequate to stimulate the development of modern nation states.

In most situations, however, it became apparent that the transformation of traditional systems into nation states would require more basic changes. Hence the second stage, when stress on a legal system was pushed to the point of establishing the machinery for the maintenance of law and order. Political development was assumed to coincide with administrative development—the characteristic rationale, of course, of colonialism.

We must pause to give special attention to this phase. It is of profound significance that the overriding stress in all Western efforts to make traditional societies into nations has been in the sphere of developing administrative capabilities. During the era of colonialism it was universally assumed that the process of political development involved primarily the creation and the effective operation of the authoritative instruments of the modern state. Whatever other motives were present, it was always believed that the highest expression of enlightenment was to be found in efforts to provide a society with efficient, competent, and rational administration. Political development meant the suppression of all irrationalities, emotionalisms, and wildly contending forces, in favor of coldly efficient, intelligent, and farsighted management of public affairs.

The notion that nation-building should properly follow up the development of competent administration remains in the philosophy behind much of the American foreign aid efforts. In seeking to help others become nation states Americans also have assumed that the heart of the problem lies not in the formalities of the legal system but in the realm of public administration and in the creation of a competent civil service. Both historically under colonialism and today through the weight of American aid programs, the West has been overwhelmingly identified with efforts to strengthen the authoritative structures of government.

Only gradually are we coming to realize that civil administration, like the legal system, furnishes too narrow an approach to the task of nation-building. There is a more fundamental level to the nation-building process—the level of creating coherent political forces which can make meaningful a people's feeling of association with their polity. We are beginning to realize that, just as it was once necessary to go beyond the formalities of legal systems and build up administrative capabilities to maintain law and order and advance public policies, so now it is necessary to go beyond instilling administrative skills and techniques and strive to shape the political context underlying formal governments.

2

This history of attempts to make all societies into nation states has been a long one, and it is important to have a clear sense of where we stand in this process. It is particularly important to realize that the West has long focused on the development of the administrative arts as a prerequisite to nation-building. We are only just beginning to realize that in the next stage in the development of a universalized nation-state system there is a far larger and more difficult task of developing political arts appropriate to nationhood.

Once the problem has been formulated in these terms, it becomes peculiarly disturbing to those who pride themselves on understanding that the informal is more fundamental in government, to realize that historically the West has been mainly concerned with the formal structures of government. Indeed, to a degree that is puzzling in the light of modern political theory, we have left to chance the creation of the political bases of national politics.

This pattern of development suggests that the West has had an extraordinary faith in the powers of spontaneity in the building of nations. Basic to the most enlightened colonial policies was the expectation that if a people were given "good government," defined in administrative terms, they would eventually appreciate its wonders and develop automatically an intelligent political process which would fully support the essentials of rational administration. Likewise, American policies toward the ending of colonialism have been profoundly colored by the belief that, once arbitrary and external restraints have been removed, a subjugated people will quite spontaneously develop democratic forms. We often feel that our kind of democracy is the most "natural" thing in the world and that, since we as a people are so inherently likeable, all others, if given the chance, will automatically emulate our ways.[1] Policy wise all that we have felt to be necessary in assisting the newly independent countries has been to rectify the deficiencies of colonial policies. Thus we began the post-colonial epic with the belief that marginal assistance, almost entirely in the realm of administration, should be enough to set the stage for the spontaneous development of democratic practices. Thus we began with Point Four, with technical assistance, and gradually we saw that the task called for more capital assistance; but now we are wondering whether we can ever be effective if we remain within the bounds of administrative programming.

It would be unjust to be overly critical of American policy makers, for they have been remarkably quick to shed their preconceptions and to try to adjust to the demands of reality. The fault lies far more with the Western political theorists who have provided the ideas and concepts that have colored the vision of the policy makers. Western political theory has given shockingly little attention to rational planning in building a democratic nation state out of a traditional society, placing implicit faith in spontaneity as the prime dynamic factor in change and development.

This problem relates to some fundamental attitudes in contemporary social science. The strength of modern political science has been its essentially static bias and its concern with explaining how things actually are. Partly in response to the urge to escape the limitations of classic political philosophy, with its normative concerns, contemporary political science has tended to avoid any problem which might appear related to idealistic or utopian rather than to realistic and empirical considerations. Thus contemporary political scientists have been more inclined to describe the current operations of politics and government in transitional systems than to take a manipulative view and analyze how such systems might be changed to achieve more effectively the standards of modern nation states.

In an even more fundamental sense, modern political theory has encouraged a misplaced faith in spontaneity by its assumptions about the relationships between state and society, between formal institutions and informal patterns of behavior. A cardinal assumption of modern political science is that formal institutions are mere reflections of the fundamental values and cultural patterns of the society as a whole, and thus the kind of government a people will develop is determined by the general state of their society, their historical experience, and the interplay of contemporary social forces. This is a view which is quite inappropriate for understanding the evolution of institutions under

Western impact and under the demands that they meet the standards of the nation-state system. These are societies in which the formal institutions of government have been introduced in a completely arbitrary fashion from the outside. At present, most of the formal institutions of government throughout the non-Western world are not expressions of the particular values and cultures of the society. The structure, form, and operations of the modern nation state are not "natural" products of most societies, but can develop only through the interactions of separate societies with the nation-state system operating as an external force.

To sum up, the process of nation-building in the new states usually began with the establishment of the legal and administrative structures of modern government, but with little attention to how these might relate to political processes which would make them responsive to political forces in the society. In most cases every effort was made to isolate the operations of government from any contact with what might be considered potential political forces, and little attention was given to building up political forces that might assume responsibility for determining the appropriate goals of administration, while at the same time respecting the integrity of the administrative system.

3

The great problem today in nation-building is that of relating the administrative and authoritative structures of government to political forces within the transitional societies. In most ex-colonial countries there is an imbalance between recognized administrative tradition and a still inchoate political process. In Vietnam and Pakistan, for example, power and authority are centered in the realm of administrative officialdom. These structures, which were built up during the colonial period when governments were expected to rule rather than to respond to political forces, have not been effectively transformed into agents of popular, representative politics.

It may not at first seem as though the same problem could exist in countries where nationalist movements have overpowered the colonial tradition of administrative rule and in which politics unlimited seems sovereign. On closer examination, however, it becomes evident that even in such situations there has been a gross imbalance between administrative traditions and political forces, and that the assault of the politicians upon the administrative institutions is inspired by relative weakness, not strength. Where they have, in a sense, had their day of popular acceptance, nationalist movements have now settled on the easy alternative of preserving their power by crowding in on the administrative structure rather than striving to build up permanent and autonomous bases of power. The leaders of such nationalist movements have tried to achieve their destiny by politicizing, and hence corrupting, the upper reaches of the administrative structures, while allowing the mass base of their movements to wither and decline to the point that they can only be used to put on ritualistic demonstrations at times of "elections" or when foreign visitors need to be impressed. When the division between the administrative and the political is violated to such an extent, the capacity for effective administration declines and the development of political processes is also stifled.

The almost universal decline of political parties in the new states is evidence of the tendency of politicians to undermine the autonomy of administration rather than strengthen political representation. This weakening of the vitality and efficacy of political parties is, in many respects, the most ominous development in the post-colonial period. It is to be observed in countries which first seemed headed toward a multi-party system as well as in those which gained their independence under the auspices of a single nationalist movement. For example, Indonesia emerged from Dutch rule with a multiplicity of apparently vigorously contending and potentially coherent political parties which represented with reasonable accuracy the distribution of political interests and ideas of the country. Yet, within a decade, party politics is dead, administrative powers have been used to suppress some parties, and President Sukarno has even turned his back on building up his Nationalist Party in favor of ruling directly through the authoritative organs of government. In other countries, such as Burma and Ghana, the dominant nationalist party which was the vehicle of the independence movement has lost its political significance as all the leaders have gradually sought the greater security and recognized authority which comes from occupying a place in the administrative structures.

The general conclusion is unmistakable. Nation-building in the new countries has encountered serious difficulties over the problem of establishing open politics outside of the sphere of administrative operations. Only in rare cases, such as in India, has the integrity of the civil service and the vitality of the political parties been maintained to a reasonable degree; and in India there are many disturbing signs of a decline in the autonomous strength of the Congress Party and of an excessive reliance upon administrative authority by Indian political leaders. Elsewhere the general picture has been one of a decline in both the capacity to administer and the vitality of popular politics.

There is no denying the conspicuous decline in administrative effectiveness in many of the new countries. Our analysis suggests, however, that public administration cannot be greatly improved without a parallel strengthening of the representative political processes. In fact, excessive concentration on strengthening the administrative services may be self-defeating because it may lead only to a greater imbalance between the administrative and the political and hence to a greater need of the leaders to exploit politically the administrative services.

This is not the place to discuss the complex and extremely delicate interrelationships between administrator and politician, between instrumental technique and the selection of values and goals. It is sufficient to say that in any representative system, and indeed in any modern nation state which depends upon applying technology to political purpose, these two functions and roles rarely rest in easy relationship with each other. Witness the history of relations between Congress and the Executive in the United States. In many respects the relationship in a parliamentary system is even more delicate, involving as it does the intimate but status-bound relations between Minister and Chief or Permanent Secretary. Yet clearly the problem is peculiarly acute in most transitional societies, where it constitutes a major obstacle to national development.

The main difficulty, as our historical analysis has suggested, is that the role of the administrator was created in almost complete isolation from that of the politician. To an extraordinary degree in most transitional societies the administrators and the politicians have developed quite separate traditions. More important, they have little tradition of working together and often harbor memories of intense conflicts during the last stages of the colonial period.[2] On the other hand, more stable patterns of development have occurred where the politician's role was created in conjunction with that of the administrator or where there was not an exaggerated building-up of the administrative services before the establishment of a public form of politics. For example, in India the Congress Party dates back to 1885 and the Indian politician and administrator had many opportunities to learn the importance of each other's roles before independence. Similarly, in the Philippines American administrators expected political parties to assume responsibilities almost as soon as the civil service was established.

It may be argued that we have possibly idealized the separate functions of bureaucratic management and political decision-making and that we have been thinking of bureaucracy in terms of a Weberian ideal type, ignoring the extent to which all administration involves an inherently political process. The query might be raised as to whether the administrative service might not be able to perform in many of these countries the functions left to political parties in the West. Viewed in such terms the degree to which the administrative services have been "politicized" should not be seen as a cause of concern but simply as a different way of arranging the political sphere.

Unfortunately we can take little comfort from such reasoning. We are not insisting that the new countries should respect the division of powers which we have found useful, but rather that they need both effective administration and coherent political mobilization—and that they are tending to get neither. We are not suggesting that the administrative process should be devoid of politics. In many of the new countries administration would be far more effective if administrators were to adopt more aggressive measures and seek to be more political and less legalistic. Our point is only that the authoritative organs of government, weak as they are, tend to overshadow the non-bureaucratic components of the political system. Until these components

have been strengthened, the new countries will have neither
effective administration nor the bases for stable political processes.

4

We turn now to an examination of the reasons for the relative
weakness of the non-bureaucratic components of the political
system. All the reasons for weakness which we shall be citing
are related to one prime issue which rests at the heart of the
nation-building problem in most new countries. This is the
issue of the management of diversity and unity, more specifically
the need to relate the parochial and the universal, to fuse basic
components of the indigenous culture with the standards and
practices of the modern world.

It is odd that the political class in most transitional societies
fails to sense the legitimacy of the parochial in politics. Despite
all the statements about the virtues of earlier traditions, the
leaders of most transitional countries tend to feel intensely
uneasy about any tradition-motivated group displaying political
interests. Thus the validity of caste, of ethnic and linguistic
groups, is denied, and it is assumed that nation-building can
best proceed as through such differences did not exist. Parochial
interests will not, however, disappear so easily, and in various
ways they will intervene in the political process to haunt the
nationalist politicians.

The difficulty is that national leaders, and those who would
play the inner elite game of politics, feel that they must represent the nation as a whole rather than particularistic interests.
They feel that to build a modern nation they should suppress
and inhibit anything which appears to be at odds with the ideal
of a unified, modernized nation. In seeking to follow such a
course the politicians risk representing no one but their own
class. Even the administrator tends to have a clearer link with
specific interests within the society. For in many transitional
societies the administrators and government civil servants are
identified with the people who were Westernized during the
period of colonial rule. In this sense the administrators are
spokesmen of a special interest group.

Indeed in many transitional societies the clash between administrator and politician has reinforced the politician's suspicions of particular interests and encouraged him to champion a diffuse and necessarily vague concept of the national interest. The politicians can sense that the higher civil service, though a potential modernizing agent, represents in fact the values, prejudices, and ambitions of a very definite and limited stratum of the total society—the more established, Westernized, and educated families. Generally the politicians do not belong to this social class and they know that they cannot support it. Nor do they have a comparable social stratum of their own.

In other words, the emerging nationalist, and to a degree revolutionary, politicians of the new countries generally do not have strong ties with any particular segments of either the old, traditional society or the new, urbanized classes. In far too many countries the politicians at the national level lack links with the grass roots and the world of the peasant. In some cases they may find it essential to come to an accommodation with a landlord class, but this is usually not a happy or fruitful marriage. There may also be similar arrangements between politicians and individuals in the commercial and modern trading world, but generally these are not regarded as legitimate associations designed to strengthen the society and the economy.

The absence of concrete ways for fusing the parochial and the universal, the traditional and the modern, local sentiments and cosmopolitan standards, compels the politicians of many transitional societies to seek solutions by formulating ideological abstractions. A Sukarno feels compelled to talk about the need to rediscover the essence of Indonesian identity even as he undercuts the particular Indonesian groups engaged in advancing their collective identities. Many African politicians feel that they are representing the values and spirit of the parochial in their countries by turning their backs on the existing groups in their societies and joining with other politicians to search for the "soul of Africa" in the politics of "pan-African movements."

The fundamental problem of course is that in most transitional societies the process of social differentiation and specialization has not as yet reached the point of providing an adequate division of labor to give the basis for functionally specific interest groups. Yet at the same time the foundations for consensus in the traditional order have been so weakened that they are inadequate to support a new polity. In transitional societies many institutions are weak, but none are weaker than those which would articulate the diverse and competing interests of the society. The mechanisms for sifting out interests are so weak that national leaders feel compelled to act as though they were dealing with an essentially undifferentiated public.

Under these conditions politicians speak out in terms of the most general and abstract, avoiding the concrete or specific. They must seek to represent all by advancing ideologies which profess to encompass the interests of all; they must ask all the people to accept them as embodying the interests of the nation and hence the interests of all. This is the natural and easy strategy for politicians caught in such circumstances, but it is not a strategy which will foster stable representative institutions. Democratic politics must be built upon a bargaining process in which the particular interests of all are respected and in which the politician seeks to perform a brokerage role in aggregating interests into various policy mixes. Out of the tension between special and general interests arise both the dynamic basis for democratic politics and the fundamental consensus which molds diversity and flexibility into the unity and strength of a modern polity.

The inherent difficulty of relating the parochial and the cosmopolitan in most transitional societies creates within the political class a diffuse sense of distrust of all manifestations of assertive traditional life. It is here that we find the fundamental psychological source of the widespread anxiety of elites in underdeveloped societies that their countries will splinter apart over traditional communal differences. Objectively many of these societies do have ethnic and language barriers dividing their peoples into different community groupings, and there is generally little consensus about the structure and form of the national political system. It seems, however, that in most of these countries these objective problems are greatly magnified by the politician's persisting belief that any acceptance of the parochial will invite disaster. More often than not the elite is only expressing fears of losing its own dominant position. Since it has identified its own well-being with the future of the country, it tends to see any threat to itself as a threat to the unity of the country.

By using the issue of national unity to prevent the representation of particularistic groupings, the political class generally weakens the coherence of the nation and produces tensions which in turn seem to justify authoritarian practices. In some instances the pattern is that of direct suppression of opposition elements and potentially dissident groupings, as for example in Ghana and Indonesia. In others, the political elite has fallen back upon administrative rule and the inherent authority of the state apparatus.

Whenever the pressures of the parochial are too great, as for example in the agitation for linguistic states in India, and parochial interests have had to be accepted into the national political process, the result has usually been a strengthening of the national unity. In India it could be argued that most such concessions to linguistic groupings, castes and other traditional associations, have widened the range of people who have a satisfying sense of identification with the Union of India while at the same time weakening the partisan position of the Congress Party. It could be similarly maintained that in many Southeast Asian countries greater sensitivity on the part of the national elite for minority and regional interests might have reduced tensions and encouraged all groups to feel that they have a stake in the national government. It is equally clear that such concessions would have compromised the role of the particular elite group in power and weakened its claim of being the embodiment of the national interest.

This problem is closely related to the intensely politicized nature of social relations in most transitional societies. The political socialization process in most transitional societies has not instilled in people a strong sense for the distinction between the partisan and the impartial, between the political and the apolitical. In most such countries people have been trained to think about politics from an intensely partisan point of view and to reject the concept that there may be politically neutral and independent institutions. The struggle against colonialism and the morality of nationalist movements have generally taught people to see all politics as a struggle in which the gain of some is the loss for others. Such societies generally do not have the training in the nonpartisan civics common to the school system of modern states. Most do not believe in the possibility of an objective and politically neutral press, a professionalized system of mass communication, an independent judiciary, and a neutral civil service.

The American child is so politically socialized that he usually values and sees security in nonpartisan institutions and in ostensibly nonpartisan approaches to partisan politics. He wants to accept the myth of an independent press and a nonpolitical bureaucracy, and he tends to regard as cynical all suggestions that partisan considerations have affected these institutions. In contrast, the socialization process in most ex-colonial countries has instilled in the politically conscious the belief that virtue and security are to be found in a partisan point of view and that nothing in the realm of public affairs can or should be considered apolitical. We have already observed the practice of considering the civil service as representing a particular class of Westernized people. Usually the press is intimately associated with particular political groupings, and there are few significant public institutions which do not reflect the political coloration of the dominant group of politicians.

The absence of a strong feeling for the very realm of the nonpartisan and the apolitical means that people in transitional societies usually do not grasp such abstractions as the "national economy" or the "national polity." When all relations that go beyond the family, the village, and the immediately personal are seen as having a political dimension, it is difficult for people to appreciate the existence of distinct systems of social, political, and economic relations.

This problem is well illustrated by research experiences in Malaya and Burma, where it was discovered that many people who had been politically involved had little or no sense for such abstractions as a national "economy" or "polity." In their thinking, economic relations involved some people making profits at the expense of others, mainly merchants cheating customers; and political relations were seen largely as some people lording it over others. These people could not picture a neutral form of "economic development" which would improve all segments of a society. Many are therefore profoundly suspicious of the American claim of wanting to advance "economic development" in their country. In their view the only reality possible was for the United States to help some people get richer; and since they personally had no contacts with the Americans, they could only conclude that our aid was being given to others. On the other hand, the Communist approach of supporting the workers and the peasants against the bourgeoisie and the imperialists conformed to the intensely partisan way in which most of these people see all political and social relationships.

The lack of a strong sense of the impartial and the apolitical severely affects the security of the political class. In claiming a degree of legitimacy that extends beyond being merely a partisan political element, many political elites seek to pose as national institutions essential for the well-being of the country as a whole. Thus although all relationships and all institutions tend to become highly politicized and there are relatively few politically independent structures in transitional societies, the constant effort of most dominant political elements is to deny the legitimacy of all competing political forces and to claim a position which is above, and not of, politics.

5

There are, of course, numerous other sources of political instability in transitional systems, but in the main these are related to the fundamental lack of consensus, the bifurcated structure with the separate worlds of urbanized elites and peasant masses, and the basic difficulty in fusing the old and the new, the parochial and the cosmopolitan. So long as large elements of these societies do not feel that their interests are being effectively represented and so long as the elite circles feel insecure because of ineffective relationships with the masses, the conditions do not exist for stable government or for efficient public administration.

By way of conclusion it may be useful to address ourselves to the argument that rapid economic development is likely to be retarded by a pluralistic political system. There is a prevalent belief that efficiency in the allocation of resources and discipline in controlling current consumption is more likely in one-party systems where there is a minimum of competitive politics. This point of view classifies democracy as a luxury which can best be afforded only after the big push for development. This is also the argument which Indians frequently make when picturing themselves as taking on the tremendous task of raising the standards of living under the handicap of employing democratic methods.

It has been our contention that most transitional societies will realize more effective administration only if they broaden and more explicitly organize the non-bureaucratic components of the political process. We are prepared to recognize that under certain very special and limited conditions there may be some advantages in highly centralized authoritarian methods. For example, after a period of prolonged disruption, or when there are acutely conflicting objectives of development and little consensus as to ultimate goals for the society, there may be advantages in arbitrary decision-making. In general, however, these conditions do not obtain in most transitional societies, and, as we have observed, the fear of many elites about divisive forces often stems from threats to their own monopoly of power and not to the basic unity of the country. On the contrary, it can be argued that at present in most situations rapid economic growth is more likely to be stimulated by a reduction in authoritarian practices and an increase in popular participation in the nation-building process. It should be remembered that the history of most backward societies is that of authoritarian rule.

The argument for a one-party system and for administrative rule tends greatly to oversimplify the problem of economic development by assuming that development hinges largely on a more rational allocation of resources. In any society the political system must cope with a wide range of demands. Even a one-party system must expend energy and resources in dealing with such demands. It is significant that most demands do not entail issues about the allocation of material resources. Just the process of participation in a pluralistic system can satisfy the search for identity of large numbers of people and thereby reduce the number of demands which might involve economically relevant resources. On the other hand, a one-party system, oriented primarily to economic development, may find that it can take care of demands only by decisions affecting the use of economic resources. Under such conditions many groups within the society may translate their aspirations into economic terms and thus place an excessive strain on the limited resources of the country.

The goal of economic development can often be better realized if the functional requirements of the political system for integration and for adjustment are met by participation in competitive politics. When the gratification of the goals of economic development becomes also the prime means for realizing the functions of integration and adaptation, the result is likely to be a less efficient approach to the objective of development.

It is, of course, a part of the democratic ethos to believe that somehow the democratic method is less efficient than authoritarian means. For example, during the last world war the democracies constantly labored under what proved to be a gross illusion that the totalitarian states were more efficient in warmaking. Similarly, we have been inclined to suspect that the Communists must have some inherent advantages in the Cold War. At present the strong drift away from democratic practices in many new countries is frequently justified on the grounds of the supposed greater effectiveness of authoritarian forms in speeding economic development.

No useful purpose is served in minimizing the very great difficulties which confront the transitional societies in their efforts to modernize. It is, however, unfortunate that, confronted with such tremendous tasks, there has been a tendency to confuse standards and to live with illusions. To a disturbing degree the strange idea has been spread within many transitional societies that democracy is linked with inefficiency, muddled actions, and corrupt practices, while authoritarian ways are identified with clear thinking, purposeful action, and firm dedication. Politicians in many such countries have sought to justify all their weaknesses and their lack of standards on the grounds that poor performance records are proof of commitment to democratic methods.

Most transitional systems urgently need more demanding and more appropriate modern standards of performance in public roles. These standards can be realized only by the effective fusing of the parochial and the cosmopolitan so as to give meaning and identity to all who would participate in the nation-building process. Hence we return again to the theme that effective government and stable political competition call for the strengthening of the essentially popular participation components of the political systems in most transitional societies.

NOTES

1. We seem to be ambivalent on this score, and our alternative mood is one of appreciating our own uniqueness and thus feeling that no one else is really ready for or capable of truly democratic institutions. Thus we tend to vacillate between the pole of believing that others should be able to achieve democratic forms without the benefit of planning and programming and the pole of denying that others can or should ever really expect to make democracy work.

2. In many of the ex-colonial countries the administrative class has been viciously attacked by the nationalist politicians as men who collaborated with the foreign rulers and worked against the nationalist movements. We shall return to this issue of loyalty and national identity in the struggle between administrator and politician; it is also treated in much greater detail in its manifestations in Burmese development in my study *Politics, Personality and Nation Building: Burma's Search for Identity* (New Haven: Yale University Press, 1962).

III

Governmental Organization and Methods in Developing Countries

JAY B. WESTCOTT

A RECENT STUDY covering over one-half the civil agency employees of the United States national government found that between 1947 and 1958 the output per person increased by 2.2 per cent a year. The per employee productivity increase in the private sector in the same period was estimated at 3.1 per cent annually.[1] These figures reflect part of a long-term trend in America; output per man-hour in 1956 was five times as large as output in 1880.[2]

In the fourteen years since independence India and Pakistan have initiated major efforts to improve productivity. Their present and future five year plans set goals for still more rapid increases. The Pakistani production targets provide for an annual growth rate of 4 per cent in the second Plan period (1960-65), 5 per cent in the third Plan period, and 6 per cent in the fifth Plan period.[3] In India for the period 1961 to 1981 the cumulative rate of economic growth will have to be 6 per cent per annum if Plan objectives are to be met.

These ambitious goals cannot be achieved without vigorous and dynamic management at all levels of government—from top to bottom. Such administrative skill does not now exist, and progress in improving governmental management has been slower than in the private sector.

India and Pakistan not only typify the management problems but also the attitudes toward such problems in most economically underdeveloped countries. Rarely is the magnitude of the managerial and technical task appreciated. The general public, the politicians, and even some top administrators grossly oversimplify the problems of management, assuming that development goals will be self-executing. There is surprise and disappointment when projects take much longer, cost far more, and result in lower quality output than planned. In fact, inadequate managerial capacity is probably the biggest single obstacle to development.

The quality of a country's administration depends largely on the general level of literacy. In countries with a high literacy level there are sufficient "support personnel," i.e., middle managers, lower-level supervisors, and workers, to meet the demands of top leadership. In countries with a low literacy rate top leaders and top administrators appear to be in fairly adequate supply; but there are not enough qualified support personnel to carry out the programs devised at the top.

In India and Pakistan nearly all of the top government administrators have been recruited from among the ablest university graduates. Many have also studied or traveled in Europe and America. Moreover, facilities to advance their skills through mid-career education and training have been expanded during the past decade. Most of the support personnel, however, have had no such well-rounded background. Their general education may have been meager; and their mid-career training opportunities have not kept pace with either the training programs for the higher-level officials or the new problems of development administration. Opportunities for up-dating their skills have either been entirely nonexistent or inadequate in terms of the Plan goals. The problem in such low-literacy countries is to widen the education base as quickly as possible.

This essay examines the dimensions of public administration deficiencies in India and Pakistan and the improvement efforts which have been made since 1947. The study of particular measures in Pakistan and India suggests ways in which the general problem of inadequate public administration in underdeveloped countries can be approached more effectively.

Public Administration Problems in India and Pakistan

Several comprehensive governmental as well as private surveys of public administration have been made in India and Pakistan since 1947. The studies represent the views of Indian, Pakistani, British, and American analysts. For example, Paul Appleby, dean of the Maxwell Graduate School of Citizenship and Public Affairs at Syracuse University, made two such surveys, in 1952 and

1955.[4] He concluded that the major reason for shortfalls in Indian development programs was administrative inefficiency. There is a surprising consensus among the recent studies and among those prior to 1947 as to the nature of the problems. Some of the more important problems are summarized below.

Inadequate attention to middle- and lower-level administrative problems. The social-intellectual orientation of the university-educated, administrative elite tends to isolate them from the detailed problems of "support management." The elite usually move directly from the university environment into the top administrative structure with, at best, only a vicarious understanding of the problems of middle and lower management.

There is also a tendency to look down upon, and therefore avoid, work in private or public development enterprise. In a recent study on nationalized industries, G. L. Sapru commented:

> In the case of India, one of the troubles is that still the Civil Service has a fascination for the young men in the Universities. The tendency is to prefer the Indian Administrative Service to even technical lines. . . . The general tendency in India is to prefer a government job with comparatively a smaller income to a job of greater emoluments in a private business concern. As such, the Government of India will have to fight this tendency, and to try to get a sizeable proportion of good personnel for the Public Enterprise.[5]

A related problem is the comparatively low social and administrative status of scientists, engineers, and others whose professions are based in the physical sciences. Although Five Year Plan goals depend heavily on their skills, the specialists are still accorded second-class rank within the governmental structures. L. Parnwell observed that scientists and technicians

> . . . have had what might be called "a bad press." Thus they have been referred to as having a narrow viewpoint of looking at business through coloured spectacles, of being excessively preoccupied with particular phases of problems and of hankering after freedom from constraint.[6]

The problem of obtaining adequate support for the scientist-engineer-technician component of society is discussed in Pakistan's *Second Five Year Plan:*

Proper recognition has not been given to the urgent need for attracting high technical talent to meet the expanding requirements of a modern administration. Status and salaries offered by the Government to technicians are well below their market value; there is serious danger that if this state of affairs continues, the vast development programmes that are being increasingly undertaken in the public sector will greatly suffer in execution. Consideration should be given to the constitution of well-paid, superior Central services, with prospects of a good career, which will provide strong and competent cadres to serve the higher technical needs throughout the country.[7]

Excessive centralization of authority and control. The gap between the qualifications of top administrative elites and lower-level personnel is at the root of many weaknesses in administrative processes. High-level officials distrust the judgment of lower-level managers and, therefore, try to do work which should be done by their subordinates. Project approvals are slowed down in the bottlenecks of top-level review. Mr. Gladieux summarized this problem as follows:

> The system is founded on belief in the infallibility of judgment if taken at sufficiently high levels no matter how far removed from the scene of action or the situational facts.
>
> The system may well have been successful in achieving its main objective of guaranteeing a sober and conservative decision making process for orthodox governmental functions. [It] . . . simply does not meet the requirements of modern government where quick and decisive action is called for day by day frequently on highly technical subjects. The slow and methodical routines . . . of papers passed up from below in a long and tenuous chain of command represents the antithesis of the dynamic administration called for by a viable nation.[8]

Finance ministries exercise detailed control requiring operating officials to justify even small expenditures.[9] As a result of this centralization major economic and welfare activities are often seriously delayed:

> . . . delegations of financial authority to the ministries and to high-ranking and responsible administration officers are negli-

gible and insignificant. . . . The result is that executive officers have to obtain sanctions—a time-consuming process—for the execution even of minor works, which should undoubtedly be within their competence to undertake.

. . . The present conception of control extends also to the examination of technical details of developmental schemes and works programs, even though the Finance Department is not properly equipped for this purpose. As a result, the objections raised are often elementary and uninformed in character. This not only acts as an irritant, but is also time-consuming. Ultimately these objections mostly come to be waived, but often after interminable discussions . . .[10]

In Indian programs for city water supply and sanitation development,

. . . the procedure adopted results in a belated information to the State Governments regarding available funds for any year. This leaves the state public health engineering authority very little time to plan for the projects, procure materials and incur the expenditure. . . . Most of the state public health engineers feel that they could handle a much larger workload, if they had advance information about specific allotments forthcoming for each year . . .[11]

Insufficient middle-level personnel. Inadequate attention is given to the need for more, as well as better trained middle-level managers and specialists. Many officials tend to judge personnel requirements by the numbers needed during the colonial law-and-order period. A Pakistan government report in 1953, for example, considered a central governmental organization of 50,000 somewhat excessive for a nation of 80,000,000 people.[12]

In 1953 Appleby considered the problem of mid-level understaffing sufficiently serious to warrant a major recommendation. He proposed:

Filling in the administrative hierarchy by making hierarchies have a more truly pyramidal form, with more executives at most levels, and by increasing the number of levels and narrowing the present excessively wide gaps between all but the low levels. This will mean more middle grade personnel and a wholly new set of titles.[13]

Appleby noted a tendency to add employees horizontally at the top levels of government rather than vertically under a system of direction and supervision:

> The phenomenon I am discussing is a hierarchal structure not filled-in, not having much pyramidal form. It leads to a high-level lateral proliferation of structure into new ministries, new departments, and "attached" organizations, making the jobs of ministers and secretaries less and less manageable. More of the lateral proliferation ought to occur at lower levels. There ought also to be a substantial increase in hierarchal depth.[14]

An example of this kind of improper structuring and misuse of the "span of control" concept may be noted in a recent description of the Indian Ministry of Foreign Affairs:

> A branch which is normally under the charge of an Under Secretary consists of two sections. Two branches ordinarily constitute a division which is normally under the charge of a Deputy Secretary.[15]

Inadequate contact between managers and subordinate employees. Most, or all, contemporary books on administration suggest that managers and supervisors should spend a substantial portion of their time guiding the activities of subordinates. To be effective, managers and supervisors need to become familiar with subordinates' activities through group meetings, individual discussions, informal visits to the subordinates' work places, and other two-way exchanges of information.

Vertical relationships in the public administration of India and Pakistan are largely limited to the flow of documents and occasional formal directives or requests by top officials. Lack of personal contact between contiguous vertical levels means that there is little understanding of one another's problems or of potentials for production and improvement. Where personal contact exists, the relationship may be negative. Mr. L. Parnwell reports instances in which

> Some clerks who attempted to explain their work during the investigation gave a distinct impression of keenness and intelligence, but the testy reaction of more senior clerks to their efforts was sometimes depressing.[16]

Excessive paper processing. Most observers have concluded that systems of processing official papers are cumbersome and antiquated. Appleby discovered

> . . . from 30 to 42 different handlings of a letter when the letter was given consideration only within a single department of a ministry; six of these handlings are required in a single office at six different points in the process, four in each of two other offices, and from 12 to 18 different officers were involved in the whole process, not including the central dispatch office. In addition, records and indexing appear to be entered in journal-type books, . . .[17]

Similarly, Parnwell observed that in East Pakistan ". . . there is a clerk for every two or so papers entering an office daily."[18]

Both India and Pakistan presently use a "case file" system of paper processing in which each subject requiring decision has its own cardboard folder or file. Every office possibly interested in the subject studies the folder to determine whether there exists a precedent or regulation which might affect the decision. The process of passing a folder from office to office frequently takes several months.

Some analysts recommend abolition of the case file system. As early as 1920 a procedures committee headed by Llewellyn Smith concluded that the defects of the case file system ". . . are so grave that if we saw another effectual remedy for them we should not hesitate to recommend the abolition of the present system." The Pakistan Administrative Enquiry Committee (1953), referring to the Smith committee, concluded:

> We are fully convinced that a further third of a century's experience has proved that, in spite of the advantages of the system, it is such a source of delay, and temptation to officers who cannot make up their minds to pass on responsibility, that it must cease. We recommend the total abolition of the present system and its replacement by self-contained memoranda.[19]

In India, Mr. Chanda suggests that a new system ". . . deserves to be introduced on the model of the system which prevails in other progressive countries."[20]

Need for greater responsiveness to the citizen's needs. The idea of a "welfare state" suggests a government which is humanely responsive to the individual and collective needs of its citizenry. The practice in India and Pakistan falls somewhat short of this ideal. There is a rather widespread feeling that the ordinary citizen cannot expect a reasonable response to requests for information or service. The Administrative Enquiry Committee in Pakistan in 1953 concluded that

> Throughout government we regret to notice a deplorable tendency to casual and even discourteous treatment of members of the public; and we feel that strong measures are called for to teach all government servants the need for courtesy and promptness.[21]

In India A. D. Gorwala observed:

> Delay in the despatch of business contributes further to public dissatisfaction. The ordinary citizen gets very tired of having to wait for an answer. . . . A certain amount of dilatoriness is inherent in the system, but it cannot be denied that a great deal of the dilatoriness so bitterly complained against is due to those working the system rather than to the system itself. When to delay is added as often happens, lack of personal touch, lack of explanation of the reasons for refusing to take certain action, the dissatisfaction is naturally greater. . . . The problem, it is felt, is essentially ethical.[22]

Parnwell suggests that much of the problem is due to misassignment of personnel which ". . . leads to masked idleness—since a table piled with files may well seem to be the best insurance against loss of employment." Complaints of lack of service only compound the difficulty; they ". . . form a considerable part of the total flow of papers, and cause a worsening of an already bad situation."[23]

Unnecessary secrecy. Larger portions of regular civil governmental affairs are considered secret than in most western democracies. Even many books and periodicals published under governmental auspices have a restricted distribution. For example, the first (1959) printed journals of the Indian National Academy of Administration were distributed to such a small clientele that Prime Minister Nehru questioned the wisdom of this restrictive policy. Paul Appleby earlier commented:

> The new government has not yet got away from an arbitrary secrecy unnecessarily depriving Indian university professors and citizens generally of desirable information. I have been privileged to see materials published "for official use only" and find often that even these are not prepared in sufficiently useful terms.[24]

In Pakistan many valuable books and articles of a general research character, as well as official documents which would be useful to scholars, journalists, and the general public are kept in official government files. Such policies deprive government of the substantial benefits of public analysis and suggestion.

Lack of line-and-staff organization. In India and Pakistan, organizational relationships have not been adequately delineated between "line" operations and the "staff" functions of personnel, budgeting and management improvement. There are only a few financial, personnel, and management specialists who can provide high-level advisory skills which expedite the work of line officials, and these existing few are not properly used. Instead, line officials become unduly involved in these staff functions about which they know only a little. Thus the functions are poorly performed and the line functions suffer from reduced leadership. This subject has been well discussed in The Pakistan Enquiry Committee report of 1953:

> Finally, there is a matter of some delicacy, but of great importance, to which I must refer because it forms part of my general scheme for clearing the ground and leaving the higher officers of Government free to devote practically the whole of their energies to their public functions. Much of the time of officers, from highest to the lowest, is at present occupied with the affairs of their own employees—their recruitment, appointment, pay, promotion, transfer, discipline and conditions of service generally, as well as with the "grievances" of individuals. It is necessary work; there are aspects of it which are of great importance and must remain the direct concern of Government, especially at a time when so much

is heard about corruption in the Services; but much of it can hardly be called "public" business.[25]

There may be some doubt that line-and-staff systems of organization could be substituted for the present structure and methods. Many Indian and Pakistani studies do not even refer to the line-and-staff idea. Paul Appleby points out that the Indians have no terminology to describe the distinctions between line and staff. None of Appleby's twelve 1953 recommendations was addressed to this fundamental structural problem—perhaps because of the difficulties and sweeping implications of any change to a line-and-staff system.

Chanda, however, believes that some change is long overdue:

A comprehensive review has yet to be attempted, even though it is generally recognized that the inherited organization is neither adequate nor appropriate for fulfilling the needs of a government which has a fundamentally different character and ideology from the previous administration. . . . Without a major readjustment of the machinery of government and a reorganization of the superior services to foster the growth of the feeling that all officers are equally responsible for the administration of the country, it would be difficult, if not impossible, to secure the fulfillment of the purposes of the state.[26]

A less ambitious approach to the development of a line-and-staff system is the Pakistani fiscal reform of July 1, 1960. Under this reform, each ministry has a fiscal officer to advise the minister. Such a reform is easier to announce than apply, but it appears a step in the right direction.

Superfluous committees and meetings. In almost all large organizations in the world, meetings are one of the main time-consumers. The problem of determining whether such meetings are productive or wasteful is not insignificant. In both India and Pakistan, committees and meetings are overused. An observer recently attended two, morning-long, official meetings of the Central Government of East Pakistan. Thirty-five officials attended one, forty-seven the other. The observer estimates that over 75 per cent of those attending learned nothing which could be used in their work.

Chanda points out that high-level committees are used in India as a substitute for good organization and coordination:

> Appointments to these [high level] committees have been made more on personal considerations than on the considera- tion of bringing only the ministers concerned together in relevant committees. A better solution might well be to in- troduce decentralized co-ordination by grouping ministries with inter-related functions together and placing these groups under the general supervision of senior ministers . . .[27]

Need for consistency in promotions, incentives, and encourage- ment of initiative. At the highest levels of public administration (the Indian Administrative Service and the Civil Service of Pakistan) officers are carefully nurtured throughout their careers. Superior intelligence, initiative, and hard work are recognized and rewarded. Relatively little attention is given to encouraging lower-level employees (e.g., Class II executives and Class III clerical employees.) In-class salary increases are small and based more on seniority than performance. There is little monetary or other incentive to work especially hard or distinguish one- self. Systems of recognition and promotion are urgently needed. As Gorwala has written:

> It is very desirable that people in the lower grades of the public service should be given adequate opportunities to prove their fitness for more responsible work. . . . What is necessary is to evolve a system by which those amongst the lower ranks who are fit for higher positions can be discovered and ap- pointed. Generally this must be before the age of 35, for other- wise the habit of looking to superiors for orders becomes too deeply engrained to enable even good mental capacity to accept responsibility. Opportunities for further education must be made available in the form of special classes etc. for the younger members of the lower ranks of officials.[28]

Appleby considers personnel development at lower levels to be one of the two or three keys to effective administration in India:

> The development of lower-ranking personnel here is es- pecially crucial if future governmental needs are to be well met. And such development requires more than in-service

training; it requires a structure in which mild but frequent promotions to higher responsibilities can provide something. . . In other words, apart from an adequate general policy office not yet developed here, I think that structure and personnel management are the two major elements of concern here, and that they are mutually dependent.[29]

Inattention to production standards and quality standards. In Indian and Pakistani public administration too little attention has been given to establishing and maintaining systems to control the volume and quality of production. Work drifts through established channels without the use of schedules geared to planned output goals. In the absence of adequate incentives and training, quality standards are also difficult to establish or administer. Occasionally, individual senior officers have devised their own methods for controlling the quantity and quality of their immediate assistants' work. These isolated cases only serve to highlight the general deficiency.

Until recently Indian and Pakistani public administration literature rarely mentioned quality and quantity standards. One of the few references was A. D. Gorwala's study on *The Efficient Conduct of State Enterprises.* Modern scientific management, he commented,

> . . . is very little known in this country where efficiency, even in reputed concerns, is based generally on rule of thumb and continuous supervision. One of the principal tasks . . . should be the introduction of "scientific management." . . . "Production must go on" should be the motto and all problems the management faces will have to be from that angle.[30]

IMPROVEMENT OF ORGANIZATION AND METHODS OFFICES

The widespread administrative weaknesses in developing countries require massive improvement efforts. Every operating official bears a responsibility to improve his own organization, but he cannot do the job alone. Most countries have set up Organization and Methods (O&M) offices which provide management assistance for the bureaucracy. But a real problem comes in staffing such offices. From experience in the United States and in some other countries, at least one full-time O&M

analyst for every 1,000 employees would appear to be a minimum staffing ratio.

Most developing countries have only begun to staff O&M offices adequately, and Pakistan and India are typical. Pakistan had only sixteen O&M analysts in the central and provincial governments in 1960. In the union and state governments of India the trained analysts in 1962 numbered approximately one hundred. In Pakistan the Efficiency and O&M wings have concentrated primarily on top-level reorganization problems and improvements which have been announced by the president since 1959. The procedural and other problems of thousands of lower-level personnel have hardly been considered.

The outlook in India is somewhat brighter. On Paul Appleby's recommendation the government has established some seventy O&M offices. Staffing of these offices has so far emphasized quality and it is now felt that they have a sufficiently strong base for quantitative expansion. In 1962 it appeared likely that India would soon achieve a one to one thousand staffing ratio. The government reportedly planned to triple the number of analysts trained between early 1962 and the end of 1963.

Indian O&M offices conduct three broad types of study. First, pilot studies are made of problem areas having a potential for government-wide application. One recent example is the pilot study of reports required by government from Indian business organizations. The textile industry was selected for study. In a seven-mouth analysis conducted by three people, it was possible to reduce the number of government reports from 324 to 160. This represents an estimated annual saving of four tons of paper and the work of 200 government clerks.

A second type of study is comprehensive work analysis of large government offices, geared to streamlining operations and reducing personnel requirements. In one typical study the staff was reduced from over 700 employees to less than 500 with an accompanying improvement in work flow and office effectiveness. Inasmuch as this office was located outside India, this study also produced savings in foreign exchange. The Special Reorganization Unit of the Ministry of Finance which conducts these studies has some twenty analysts and can study only a small fraction of all governmental organizations.

The third class of study involves the preparation of construction standards for use in Five Year Plan projects. Nearly 50 per cent of Plan expenditure is for construction, and as early as 1956 the Planning Commission officially recognized that enormous amounts of resources could be saved by improving project procedures and standards. Pursuant to a 1956 directive to establish enforceable standards, the Committee on Plan Projects of the Planning Commission has published over a dozen reports on construction standards. The subjects covered include:

minor irrigation projects
office buildings and other multi-storeyed buildings
grain storage structures
government training institutes
school buildings
slum clearance and reconstruction
residential buildings
water supply and sanitation
general concepts of construction cost reduction.[31]

The reports propose corrective standards to reduce ineffective space planning, waste of construction material, and poor construction scheduling. According to the reports, savings of 15 to 50 per cent or more can be realized by careful application of the new standards.

Aside from efforts to enforce the new standards by administrative review of proposed projects, the Planning Commission has initiated O&M courses for engineers. Government engineers from all parts of India have been assembled for seven-week, full-time training, stressing the new cost reduction standards of the Planning Commission.

To call attention to the wide range of general administrative weaknesses, the government of India has produced several policy statements, procedural documents, and training manuals.[32] Pamphlets have been published on

delegation and control techniques for achieving better administration;
improved systems of programming for public works, i.e., "the line of balanced technology";
inventory control;
maintenance of motor vehicles.

A journal entitled *Work Improvement* has been published bimonthly since September, 1961, by the Organization and Methods Division of the Cabinet Secretariat. Most of the articles are written by government officials about practical problems of middle management. Subjects covered include: "Steps to Self-improvement—Time Budgeting," "A B C of O&M Report Preparation," "House Keeping Sections—A Work Study," "Registration of Incoming Communications," "Flow Process Charts—Their Uses in Administrative Analysis," "Records Management," and "Higher Efficiency in Office Work Through Training on the Job."

The most comprehensive Indian training document on administration improvement is a 250-page draft manual on "administrative research" which is the basic text for in-service training of O&M analysts.[33] Technically, this manual compares favorably with training manuals on administrative improvement prepared elsewhere in the world. Its special advantage for India and for other newly independent countries is that it is oriented towards administrative problems peculiar to economically underdeveloped countries, and is adaptable to O&M training in other developing countries. The titles of the fourteen chapters of the manual are:

1. Introduction to administrative research and work study
2. a. Scope of administrative research
   b. Administrative survey methods
3. Elements of administration
4. Organization analysis
5. Methods analysis
6. Work measurement
7. Statistical approach to administrative problems
8. a. Forms analysis and control
   b. Space lay-out and utilization
   c. Record management
9. Project preparation and analysis
10. Programme planning and evaluation
11. Inventory control
12. Cost reduction and investment decision
13. Job enthusiasm
14. Conference technique.

Indian policies for administrative improvement were summarized in a set of "Papers on Measures for Strengthening of Administration," presented to the two houses of Parliament in August 1961,[34] which provide long lists of policy statements and action programs. Among the more important guidelines, the papers list:

If speed and efficiency are desired in the Secretariat, the number of decision makers has to be increased; the methods of their work have to be changed and greater attention has to be paid to problem solving by constituting integrated groups with specific time limits to arrive at agreed conclusions.

Changes have also to be made in the structure having regard to the increasing technological bias in administration now and in the future.

The responsibility of the Head of Department and the executive authority concerned with the implementation of programmes and policies will be substantially increased.

The present system of financial control should be reorganized. . . . Financial responsibility should be devolved, in liberal measure, on the administrative ministries and by them, in turn, on the implementing authorities.

The managerial skills of the public servants will be increased through a sustained programme of executive development by training and counselling.

Simplification of procedures and work will be vigorously pursued by introducing work studies, by competently trained personnel, in all spheres of administration.

Relations with the public will receive special attention. A series of programmes will be initiated for inculcating courtesy and consideration and for changing the attitude of authority complex towards those who approach public offices for various purposes.

Officials in key posts will be kept in their jobs for at least five years to enable them to produce the results expected of them.

Resort to committees, groups, conferences, etc., should be reduced drastically. Full responsibility should be given to agencies and to individuals and, with it, the necessary measure of support and trust.

. . . planning for the Fourth Plan should be started immediately and a comprehensive time-table may be worked out for completing studies for the Fourth Plan projects during the next three years.

Management of projects is a new and important part of administrative practice. Its special features are definite targets and schedules, costing, need for initiative and resourcefulness in execution and emphasis on technical efficiency and innovation.

All major projects should have units for evaluation, review for progress, reduction of costs, raising productivity and checking of performance.

Work study will be introduced as a compulsory subject in the initial training curricula of all established services. Courses in work study for in-service personnel will also be expanded.

Training in supervisory techniques will be stepped up for all types of personnel in service.

Incentive schemes, based on systematically worked out standards, will be tried.

India has made a good start in coping with the immense problem of providing adequate public administration. But this is only a beginning. Present programs train only a few hundred officials annually and there is not sufficient variety in course material to meet the wide range of special requirements. The minds and habits of tens of thousands of workers and managers will have to be changed. What India and other countries with inadequate administrative capacity must try to achieve rapidly is a level of training which in Western industrial nations required a half-century of effort.

The Improvement Role of Training and Self-Help

The task of rapidly achieving better management in underdeveloped countries is immense but not impossible. These countries can profit from both the mistakes and the experience of the past half-century in Western industrialized countries. Today, no time lag need take place in the initiation of extensive training programs in the newer countries. In the West nearly forty years elapsed between Frederick Taylor's first published ideas on productivity (in "Shop Management," published in 1903) and World War II when it was discovered that massive training programs for supervisors and workers could lead to revolutionary increases in productive efficiency. Today's training manuals, course outlines, textbooks, and audio-visual aids are the product of millions of hours of mostly post-1945 research and experimentation. These materials are available for use in any country. Although they have to be adapted to local situations, these changes are much easier to make than the creation and testing of training materials *de nuovo*.

There is general agreement that massive training efforts cannot succeed without the support of upper-level administrators. This must be more than token support or lip service. In India and Pakistan, for example, the recent, new upper-level governmental programs could hardly have been initiated without the energetic encouragement and continued support of Prime Minister Nehru and President Ayub Khan. In many organizations it has been found helpful to give "appreciation courses" for middle-level and upper-level administrators. These courses, which last from an hour to a few days, explain briefly the general purposes and content of longer courses for lower-level supervisors and workers. Without this information, many administrators tend to underestimate the value of the training and to undercut its general usefulness.

Aside from the specialized courses in management training needed in any developing society, a few generalized courses have emerged in the United States which appear applicable in nations throughout the world. They include "executive leadership," "human relations for supervisors," and "administrative communication." One of the more successful of the general courses is "training in work simplification." It is a course in management orientation and techniques for first line supervisors; its use in many countries merits a brief description of its content and utility.

Standardized training in simplification of work methods has been given to hundreds of thousands of governmental and industrial employees since 1945. The standard course is so easy that any employee, regardless of prior education and experience, can be taught the elements of work improvement. In the typical governmental work simplification course the first line supervisor spends about four hours a week for four or five weeks studying the techniques of work improvement and applying them to the unit or section in which he works. Five techniques which each student is required to learn and apply are:

1. *Work Distribution.* How is the work divided among the employees in my unit? Can I devise a revision which will be more logical and lead to better results?

2. *Work Count.* How large is each employee's volume of work? Is the amount of work evenly distributed?

3. *Flow Process Analysis.* What is the flow of work through the unit? Can it be simplified and streamlined to eliminate unnecessary steps?

4. *Motion Economy.* Are any of the employees in the unit wasting motion in doing their work? What are the simplest possible ways to do the work?

5. *Space Layout.* Would the physical rearrangement of the people and the work lead to simplifying the unit's work?

Each person who participates in the fourteen to twenty classroom hours' study of work simplification is expected to develop at least one recommendation for work improvement before he completes the course. These recommendations are often officially adopted and put into practice. One United States government department with 450,000 civilian employees started a work simplification training program in 1952. In nine years (1952-61) over 139,000 employees, including nearly all supervisors and lower level managers, received this training. Over 77,000 improvements proposed by the students were put into effect at an average estimated saving of over $1,000 per recommendation; this department estimates its savings at over ten times the cost of the training program.

In another United States department with a work simplification training program, one employee made eighty-four usable recommendations between 1942 and 1961. For these recommendations he has received seventy-six cash rewards totaling over $5,000. This employee finished only eight years of formal education before he left school and took his first job.[35]

The most significant results from work simplification training appear to be non-monetary. In a study of seventy-five American corporations using this training, the author rated the benefits in the following order of importance:

improved human relations and attitudes
lower operating costs
less resistance to change
development of supervisory personnel
increased productivity
improved cooperation and teamwork
better employee morale.[36]

Another impressive innovation since 1945 which combines organizational self-help and self-training, is the "self-survey" of organization and management. Through use of all people in an organization, it achieves administrative improvement with a minimum of expert O&M staff. It is being used increasingly in both public and private organizations.

Self-survey is a practical application of the idea that every operating official is responsible for the effectiveness and efficiency of his organization. In the self-survey each administrator, manager, supervisor, and employee is expected to analyze the activities for which he is responsible and to propose as many improvements as possible. Thus, every member of an organization from top to bottom has a responsibility to think creatively about his work. Through discussions and central coordination these ideas are assembled into plans for general improvement throughout the organization. Usually a few outsiders are asked to evaluate a self-survey, studying the ideas developed within the organization and making comments or further recommendations. The outside participants are experienced in the kinds of work performed by the organization; thus their ideas are invaluable to the self-surveys.

In recent years, American state governments, universities, and other educational institutions have made extensive use of the self-survey.[37] Evaluations of the results of these surveys suggest several benefits:

1. They appeal to the initiative and creativity of the operating employees. The employees themselves receive credit for the improvements; thus they are more inclined to propose changes

than is the case when outside O&M specialists are responsible for recommendations.

2. They provide a basis for improved morale by bringing to light problems which may have been irritating the employees.

3. They provide an opportunity to restate long-range and short-range goals, and to relate the work of each unit to the over-all objectives.

4. They provide practical in-service education and training to managerial and supervisory personnel on a wide range of operating problems of the entire organization; thus coordination and teamwork of the organization are improved.

An experiment in the use of the self-survey was attempted as a training experience in New Delhi in 1962. Employees in the organization were already positively oriented toward the idea of work improvement, and the experimental and training purposes of the project were carefully explained. Most of the employees responded favorably, and a large number of practical suggestions were made, some of which were put into immediate effect. Representatives from Indian local government training institutes who observed the experiment believe that self-survey improvement may be especially useful in the community development environment, inasmuch as management improvement staffs are not available to make studies in the 4,000 development blocs and 585,000 villages of India.

To conclude these remarks, in the first decade after independence, officials in India and Pakistan began to recognize the complexity of the administrative deficiencies which were retarding economic development. Steps to improve public administration were suggested by a succession of *ad hoc* committees and foreign consultants but little progress was made toward correction. In the second decade more extensive improvement efforts are under way. In the Planning Commissions, in project control offices, and in O&M offices, analysts have been hired to make systematic studies and install improved procedures. Experience shows that these efforts are still too small to bring about broad-scale, rapid improvement. Nevertheless a base exists from which expansion of systematic improvement efforts could take place.

Beginnings are also being made in management improvement

training programs for governmental employees. A few courses have been set up especially for upper-level administrative officials, and some good training literature has been produced. Nevertheless, these efforts have been too restricted to reach more than a small percentage of employees who need the training. Simple, short, in-service courses which could be given to thousands of employees have not yet been exploited; nevertheless it is among these people that dramatic improvements could be achieved.

Two negative generalizations may be made from the management improvement experience of India and Pakistan since independence:

1. There is a tendency for people to assume that the operating dimensions of development administration are relatively simple and that the fruits of a better society will flow from national independence and high social purpose;

2. Once operating difficulties are encountered, there is a tendency to assume that a relatively small amount of effort will provide the correctives, after which development goals will be rapidly achieved.

The economic systems which produce high standards of human welfare, however, are actually more complex than they may appear. Social goals have to be set within the context of the environmental and human limitations of each society. Then a significant segment of the total national effort must be devoted to adapting workers at all levels of organization to the new demands necessary to relate means to ends.

NOTES

1. Henry D. Lytton, "Estimating Recent Federal Agency Productivity Trends" (unpublished monograph, 1959).

2. Committee for Economic Development, *Economic Growth in the United States* (New York: 1958), p. 31.

3. Pakistan, Planning Commission, *The Second Five Year Plan* (1960-65), p. 4.

4. Paul Appleby, *Public Administration in India—Report of a Survey* (Delhi: Manager of Publications, 1953) and *Re-examination of India's Administrative Systems with Special Reference to Administration of Government's Industrial and Commercial Enterprises* (New Delhi: Government of India, Cabinet Secretariat, Organization and Methods Division, 1956).

5. G. L. Sapru, "The Administration of Nationalized Industries in India" (Unpublished Ph.D. dissertation, Lucknow University, 1958), p. 354.

6. L. Parnwell, *Organization and Methods in the East Pakistan Government* (Dacca: East Pakistan Government Press, 1958), p. 18.

7. Pakistan *Second Five Year Plan*, p. 113.

8. Bernard Gladieux, "Reorientation of Pakistan Government for National Development" (Karachi: mimeographed, 1955), p. 68.

9. Asok Chanda, former Comptroller and Auditor-General of India, reports the case of a broken banquet table leg in an Indian embassy. Before the ambassador could have it repaired and resume official entertaining, he had to justify the wisdom of the proposed expenditure to the External Affairs and the Finance Ministries in New Delhi. See Chanda, *Indian Administration* (London: Geo. Allen & Unwin Ltd., 1958), pp. 222-23.

10. *Ibid.*

11. Committee on Plan Projects, *Report on National Water Supply and Sanitation Schemes* (New Delhi: Government of India Press, 1961), p. 16.

12. Government of Pakistan, *Report of the Administrative Enquiry Committee, 1953* (Creagh Coen Report), p. 6.

13. *Public Administration in India, op. cit.,* p. 15.

14. *Ibid.,* p. 20.

15. Indian Institute of Public Administration, *The Organization of the Government of India* (New Delhi: 1958), pp. 32-33.

16. Parnwell, *op. cit.,* p. 13.

17. *Public Administration in India, op. cit.,* p. 61.

18. Parnwell, *op. cit.,* p. 11.

19. *Report of . . . Enquiry Committee, op. cit.,* pp. 53-54.

20. Chanda, *op. cit.,* p. 160.

21. *Report of . . . Enquiry Committee, op. cit.,* p. 29.

22. A. D. Gorwala, *Report on Public Administration* (New Delhi: Government of India Press, 1951), p. 4.

23. Parnwell, *op. cit.,* pp. 10-11.

24. *Public Administration in India, op. cit.,* p. 30.

25. *Report of . . . Enquiry Committee, op. cit.,* p. 48.

26. Chanda, *op. cit.,* p. 99.

27. *Ibid.,* p. 91.

28. Gorwala, *op. cit.,* p. 49-50.

29. *Public Administration in India, op. cit.,* pp. 29-30.

30. (New Delhi: Government of India Press, 1951), p. 19.

31. Thirteen such studies were done between 1958 and early 1962.

32. Four studies on various aspects of administrative improvement were undertaken by the Organization and Methods Division and the Committee on Plan Projects in 1961.

33. "Administrative Research Training Course" (printed draft, February, 1962). The printed draft will probably be published in book form.

34. (New Delhi: Government of India Press, 1961).

35. *New York Times*, March 20, 1961, p. 17.

36. "Why Work Simplification Clicks—and Why It Fails," *Factory Management and Maintenance*, CXII, No. 11 (November, 1954), 122.

37. See, for example, Arthur Naftalin, "Minnesota Self-Survey: A Progress Report," *State Government* XXXI (Autumn, 1958), 252-260.

IV

Cultural Hurdles in Development Administration

AGEHANANDA BHARATI

CULTURAL HURDLES may be defined as the traditional attitudes or customs which are part of the cultural base in a particular region and which constitute barriers to innovation. In this study "culture" is used in the narrow sense of tradition; if everything that happened in an area were viewed as part of its culture, the concept of cultural hurdles would be meaningless. Cultural hurdles must also be distinguished from what could be called "universal psychological hurdles" which are general human phenomena and do not grow out of any specific cultural base. It is the thesis of this paper that genuine cultural hurdles to development are not very numerous in any particular region.

The following sketch of cultural hurdles on the Indian scene has a general relevance in other countries where administrators seek to promote change. Indigenous patterns of thought and tradition in a region are often ignored or misunderstood not only by alien but by native administrators. A Panjabi civil servant usually knows little more about a Kerala milieu than an American guest administrator. It matters not in what area or country the administrator is operating; failure to be aware of cultural hurdles can seriously undermine efforts, whereas familiarity with and use of cultural patterns can greatly facilitate the modernizer's task. The anthropologist can offer no cut and dried methods of procedure. However, using India as our example, we can point to pitfalls and indicate lines of approach for the administrator who seeks to shape tradition and promote change.

RELIGIOUS TRADITION AND CULTURAL HURDLES IN INDIA

In India and in other regions (e.g., Ceylon and East Pakistan) where predominant importance is given to the spiritual world, and religious tradition is the guiding reference for behavior, people may be reluctant to cooperate when innovation seems to conflict with religious tradition. Most cultural hurdles in India

68

derive from the strength of religious tradition. Mundane efforts are considered basically trivial—a powerful impediment to development administration on all levels.

Thailand provides an illuminating contrast to the Indian pattern. Though the Thais inherited a purely Indian set of moral doctrines through *Theravāda* Buddhism, religious tradition does not pose cultural hurdles for Thai development. The Siamese enthusiastically welcome innovation. They render unto Buddha what is Buddha's—concern with nirvana, etc. But while life lasts, they reason, the best should be made of it. The painful essence of life belongs in the realm of theological definition. The idea that life can be fun is definitely not Buddha's teaching but it characterizes the Thai attitude, both clerical and lay. Hence, Siamese planners and administrators do not consider that development clashes with tradition nor is development administration considered trivial.[1]

It is obvious that cultural hurdles must be evaluated in terms of specific areas and situations. General standards for evaluation must be given situational content. The present study is directed toward actual or potential reactions of Indian (Pakistani or Ceylonese) individuals or groups in contact with native or foreign development administrators. The situation is one of unprecedented effort to introduce innovation in a specific cultural milieu where novel administrative patterns cannot be or are not wholly absorbed.

In India most cultural hurdles can be related to a traditional lack of secular institutions. Historical accident, not something innate in the Indian national character or in any of the indigenous religious traditions, accounts for this lack of secular institution building. All Indian traditions distinguish between two totally different and unconnected realms of truth and existence—the phenomenal or ephemeral world, and the absolute un- and anti-worldly universe. Individuals or groups are respected and influential because of their identification with the spiritual world. In ancient Greece and Rome, and in seventeenth and eighteenth century England and Germany, absolutist philosophers looked down upon lay commoners, minimizing their intellectual importance and even their integrity. But philosophical or religious censure never inhibited the lay European's zeal for secular activity. The lay Indian institution builder, on the other hand, has been and remains profoundly affected by the absolutists' scoffs.

There have been secular institutions in all periods of Indian history, but spiritual institutions and conceptions have always been the cynosure of the Indian scene. Rulers of the state of Rajasthan call themselves *vazīr*, i.e., "representatives" of the tutelary diety.[2] While in Western dynasties such titles are just ornamental, they have very direct and real importance in India. The king who renounces the throne and becomes an itinerant saint is the ideal. If a king or a ruler or a minister does not turn completely toward the spiritual world in his later days—and very few actually did—he is conscious of his omission and his people are equally conscious of it. Orthodox Hindus praise Gandhi for his spiritual, ascetic way of life, and they blame Nehru for not regarding the spiritual as the intrinsic goal of life.

Injunctions or codes of religious tradition have a direct relation to administrative efforts in India. Individuals or groups may either *believe* a novel situation to be incompatible with tradition or a situation may be objectively incompatible. Indian legislation extending educational opportunities is objectively incompatible with traditional patterns. According to scripture only twiceborn males may study canonical literature. Recent legislation has done away with exclusion from any branch of learning because of sex, caste, or creed. All now may study the *Veda* (Hindu Scripture) and are indirectly encouraged to do so. Actually, the new legislation has left behavior substantially unchanged because very few scheduled class Hindus would embark on the study of the *Veda*. Though university students of all castes in India study Sanskrit, including the *Veda*, such texts are approached as literature, not as religious tracts.

Cases in which innovations are *believed* incompatible with religious tradition far outnumber cases of actual incompatibility. In many regions there is a wide gap between knowledge of codified tradition and the general image of the tradition. The strength of imagined incompatibility diminishes in emancipated regions. In any region, however, only theological or academic audiences would demand specific illustrations of codes which conflict with a particular development proposal. A rhetorical appeal to the spirit of a tradition is a powerful instrument. Individuals or groups central to an administrative effort may believe or claim to believe that an innovation conflicts with scriptural or oral tradition. Most political leaders assume somewhat naively that because they are inspired, they know the tradition which inspired them. The development administrator must obviously be able to cope with such flat assertions if he is to get anything accomplished.

Aside from specific religious injunctions and codes which objectively or subjectively conflict with innovation, tradition gives rise to patterns of thought which can seriously interfere with development. In some cases what might be considered universal psychological hurdles take on a peculiar manifestation in the specific cultural milieu. Take, for example, a situation in which Indian farmers or members of the *panchāyat*[3] must cooperate in setting up a power station to provide electricity and water for a number of villages. Some farming land must be used and the villagers compensated; for budgetary reasons the villagers must work for nominal wages or even without compensation. The farmers are likely to argue: "you promise us advantages x, y, and z later if we give you a, b, and c, now; but how do we know that you will bring these advantages? Rulers, parties, landowners, and their clerks also promised advantages which we never enjoyed. People act as they always have. Why should we believe you are different?" Superficially, there is nothing particularly Indian about such resistance to innovation. Yet the intensity of reaction and the form which opposition takes do have a cultural basis. A cyclical world view underlies Hindu thought on all levels of sophistication. Cyclical Hindu cosmology has even become deeply ingrained among the Muslims.[4] Everything that happens has happened before. The promises of development administrator or modernizer are no different.

Another peculiarly Indian manifestation of the universal phenomenon of resistance to change is the peasant's strong aversion to recording in secular documents anything which pertains to an individual or kin group. The Indian farmer feels that whatever is written down in an official ledger can and will later be held against him. An Indian peasant refused to sign a petition demanding diversion of an irrigation channel into an area adjacent

to his village because he "did not like to appear in writing any-
where except in the book of *Vishvanāth*."[5] Signing the *Vishvanāth,* the ledger at the famous shrine at Banaras, brought no
fear because this was a religious document pertaining to another
world.

The genuine and deep-seated fear of secular documents may
also explain why many villagers prefer the money lender to a
bank even though the former charges 100 per cent or more in
interest. Such discrepancy, the villager would reason, means the
bank must have some ulterior motive. He derives security in the
knowledge that no signature or mark must be made, no ceremony
undergone at the hands of unknown people and, most important,
no permanent record is kept of any debt.

Closely tied to religious tradition, with patterns of behavior
based on religious sanction, is the Indian caste and kinship
structure. Such traditional patterns can pose powerful cultural
hurdles. Development of radio and television educational programs in a very traditional region such as Rajasthan, for example,
might well be opposed because such innovations would influence
young people to abandon their respect for the old, members of
the lower caste groups to lose their deference for higher groups,
or women to rebel against the traditional injunction of obedience
to their husbands.

There are in all regions potential or actual hurdles which are
universal phenomena, e.g., inertia, insecurity or self-defense, unrelated to the cultural base in any but the vaguest sense.[6] In
some cases there may be initial resistance to change. For example,
if a new kind of seed, more resistant to weather and disease,
were introduced into a region confined to traditional agricultural
methods, the peasants, at least temporarily, might tend to forget
that the old seed was inferior. They might claim that the *roti*
(cappātī) made with the new wheat does not taste as good.
Such situations should not impede innovation, however, for the
peasants are soon won over by visible evidence of success.

Where tradition does not conflict or is not believed to conflict
with program administration, initial resistance can generally be
overcome by visible evidence of success. There is seldom, if
ever, continued resistance on principle to innovation, be it
administrative or technological.[7] Farmers and laborers in India

and Pakistan are eager and ready for pertinent innovations of any sort, particularly if they entail labor-saving devices. A few years ago the government of India invited a group of Japanese agricultural experts to instruct farmers in the Japanese method of rice planting by intensive soil cultivation. The method was avidly adopted by thousands of villages throughout rice-growing regions in India.

Religious tradition by no means always poses hurdles to innovation; in many cases it can be of positive benefit to modernization. Once an innovation or administrative situation is shown to be beneficial, religious teachings often encourage co-operation. Hindu scripture, for example, speaks of *niSkāma-karma* (action without the desire for its fruits), a code taken up by Gandhi and most other Hindu leaders. The second in the four stages of life in the Hindu religion, *artha,* is one of keen participation in any social activities which improve material and ideal living standards among fellow men.[8]

RELIGIOUS TRADITION AND THE DEVELOPMENT ADMINISTRATOR IN INDIA

Knowledge of the cultural processes in a region can be of positive benefit to the development administrator. A familiarity with tradition can help the administrator refine his method of introducing and encouraging support for an innovation. Traditional patterns of thought and action can often be turned from impediments into assets. Generally the methods rather than the targets of administration determine whether cultural processes will retard or facilitate development efforts. The targets are so broad and general that they can be made palatable no matter what the cultural milieu. But an agency or administrator's methods may either clash or fall in line with traditional patterns. In the Thai egalitarian tradition, for example, a charismatic figure—someone whose name is known and respected—is not required to sponsor a development effort. Government agencies could encourage development-oriented attitudes through relatively impersonal procedures. An effective hierarchy to channel information and orders from the government, ministry, or secretariat would suffice.

In India the persuasive power of the religious or charismatic leader as the traditional authority figure is essential in mobilizing popular support. Typically, a religious leader is either a *sādhu* (wandering holy man) or *āpta* (leads a professional religious life and is familiar with the codified religious tradition). In no less than five Indian movies which the author saw, a *sādhu* persuaded the people to perform necessary secular acts.[9] When Nehru's *obiter dictum,* resting is taboo (*ārām hairām hai*), was quoted at a Community Development Center meeting, the audience nodded approval. If the Panditji pronounces such a rule, it must be accepted. The charismatic figure's dictum becomes law (*shruti* in Hindu India) even though it may militate against the general temperament. Nehru is a charismatic figure, just as his preceptor has been. His words would be heeded, even though he headed a totally different government and asked support for exactly the opposite kind of policy. Since hero-worship is the dominant political practice, any leader personality—religious and secular alike—would be followed no matter what his policy or ideology. "If Nehru were the Chairman of the Indian Communist Party, he would still be the idol of the masses."[10]

Fortunately, the development administrator does not need to enlist the aid of Nehru to convince the people to cooperate on the local level. The authority of a religious scholar, respected for his knowledge of tradition is quite sufficient to persuade an apathetic or hostile audience of the need for innovation and convince doubters that there is traditional sanction for the innovation. The *āpta* does not *support* a governmental or any other policy. He states what is good, and if the governmental policy *happens* to coincide with what he states, it will be implemented, or at least there will be cooperation. The government policy and efforts to encourage are secondary in importance. The *āpta's* statement is the primary stimulus. In other words, the Hindu audience does not conceive of the sage as supporting government policy; rather, it reasons that sage X tells us a certain type of action leading to a certain achievement is good, and the government happens to want the same action; hence let us cooperate.

Occidental administrators would not think or presume to challenge the authenticity of a reference to indigenous tradition. With the help of the religious scholar, however, the development administrator might soon find that Hindu tradition actually poses fewer barriers to modernization than most Hindus think or care to know.[11] The administrator himself cannot convince an audience that an innovation is only *believed* incompatible with tradition. For example, members of Indian Parliament recently strongly objected to a proposal that the government disseminate information on birth control on the grounds that contraception was contrary to Hindu scriptures and repugnant to the "spirit" of Hindu tradition. Here was a case of rhetorical appeal to *believed* tradition. The leader of the Communist Party in the House pointedly noted: "It is regrettable that there is no Hindu scholar here who would show that Hinduism does not object to birth control."[12] Only a religious scholar could effectively challenge objectors to point out scriptural or other codes which they call "our tradition" or the "spirit" of our tradition.

An *āpta* or *sādhu* could also be enlisted to demonstrate that a proposed change is compatible with tradition; scripturally uninformed yet orthodox Hindus then generally accept almost any innovation with relative ease. The Mazhampula Dam in Kerala, for instance, was pictured by a *sādhu* as fulfilling an aspect of the Hindu *shāstras* (i.e., the written canonical tradition). The *sādhu's* statement was sufficient encouragement for the initially reluctant.

In 1938 Mr. Gandhi intensified his efforts to convince Hindus that outcastes were entitled to all benefits then reserved for caste Hindus. Non-caste Hindus, like non-Hindus, were barred from worshipping at most Hindu shrines. This question of temple-entry, incidentally, has not been completely settled even today. Mr. Gandhi called upon a learned pandit whose views were quite radically divergent from those of other orthodox scholars. Accompanying the Mahatma to a lecture before an audience of learned Brahmins, the scholar "quoted" scripture in support of Gandhi's view that *Harijans* (People of God, the Gandhian term for outcastes) could enter and worship in temples. The Brahmins were convinced.[13]

The savant later confided that he had quoted non-existent passages which he had composed in Vedic Sanskrit for the occasion. To most Western observers as well as to Indian and other non-westerners trained in an occidental ethic, this procedure might seem morally suspicious if not downright condemnable. For the orthodox Hindu, on the other hand, this action was morally unassailable because it furthered the cause of the scriptures in the long run as a *lokahitārtha* ("for the benefit of the world" strategem).[14] The *lokahitārtha* is well established as a scriptural vindication of courses of action directed toward a morally desirable end.

The *lokahitārtha* is often used to justify compromise between tradition and the demands of modernization. For example, a large section of a valley in the South Indian state of Andhra had to be flooded to build a reservoir for irrigation. An old Buddhist and Hindu shrine was located in the area. Destruction of any Hindu or Buddhist shrine is an abomination to the Hindu. (One of the main reasons for Hindu hatred of early Muslim conquerors was the desecration of Hindu shrines.) There were learned and not so learned arguments for and against flooding the temple site. The state and national Parliaments and local and central ministers regretted the necessity of destroying the shrines. Progressively oriented pandits argued that the destruction was *lokahitārtha*. When the flooding actually took place, there was little complaint. The Archaeological Survey of the central government removed virtually all the objects d'art to a museum erected for this purpose and a fine book of the site and treasures was published.

CULTURAL HURDLES AND THE DEVELOPMENT ADMINISTRATOR'S TASK

It is easier to identify hurdles to development administration which derive from a specific cultural base than it is to make the concept operationally significant for administrators in any area. In this final section we shall derive several generalizations from our specific situational analysis. There are general as well as specific standards by which the administrator can evaluate cultural hurdles. Obviously general standards are few while specific standards are as numerous as the cultural patterns in any administrative area.

Administrators must keep in mind both quantitative and qualitative questions when locating and evaluating the significance of cultural hurdles. In any administrative area it is obviously necessary not only to determine how many people oppose the administrator or a proposed change, but also to gauge the strength of the opposition's influence. Resistance from a learned Brahmin or respected scholar is clearly more serious than that from the ordinary bureaucrat. Qualitative problems also involve determining whether a proposed innovation or administrative action conflicts with actual or believed tradition. Often the administrator, with indigenous help, can successfully demonstrate that a particular change is only in imagined conflict with tradition. Or though some aspects of tradition may dictate opposition to a particular change, others may well support the innovation. In India, for example, some passages from the *Veda* could be interpreted as condemning birth control while others seem to encourage this practice. In some cases cultural hurdles can be ignored without undermining the development effort. In others the administrator can circumvent an obstacle by pointing to precedent or by persuasive discourse.

In assessing the nature of culture hurdles and determining his approach, the administrator must have a fairly refined and sophisticated knowledge of the region. While he may often be charting new courses, his approach should be conditioned by informed judgement. The need for familiarity with the region is so basic that it tends to be overlooked by authors who concentrate on structural analysis. Such understanding is vital not only for the alien but for the native administrator. The mere fact of birth or of physical presence in a region does not imply knowledge about the region.[15]

The administrator cannot hope to develop the necessary understanding of any area by reading official publications or by concentrating solely upon what groups say about themselves. Indian official manuals, for example, give no indication of the contribution which the *sādhu* or Brahmin scholar can make in promoting acceptance of change. At the same time Indian government agencies deny or try to ignore the existence of caste status which significantly affects all development—economic as well as political. Equally important to remember is that one of "the people," "the man in the street," or the office worker cannot usually discern or does not speak of his own traditional attitudes or culture patterns. Members of the white collar or *bābū* class[16] in India generally do not mention their predominantly non- or anti-secular attitude, their reluctance to give moral priority to any mundane matters, including their own jobs, or their distaste of career advancement of people outside their social caste. "Getting to know the people as you work with them" without some previous study is a hazardous affair.

In understanding any region the administrator should first survey the salient culture patterns of the groups with which he has to deal. "Salient" here refers to what the learned or at least sophisticated opinion in a given society regards as important. It requires trained people from several disciplines who question many more than one or two "men in the street" to make relevant statements about a group. Sophisticated observers of Indian culture—non-Indian as well as Indian (e.g., Mino Masani, M. N. Srinivas, Iravati Karve, Morris Opler, Edward Shils, Milton Singer, etc.)—have done informed and critical analyses. Such studies give the administrator a shortcut to greater efficiency through the best possible information. The social scientist, even though he may be interested in theoretical constructs and generalizations to an extent that they are not operational for the administrator, does provide instruments whereby pitfalls can be avoided. From such studies the administrator can anticipate what obstacles to innovation may arise and chart possible approaches for avoiding them. No one can dogmatize about "national character." The facts and facets of a country's traditions and the predilections of its *dramatis personae* are accidents, but they are accidents which the administrator should know.

What the administrator reads or gathers from learned opinion will have to be supplemented by large doses of practical experience and intuition. Although learned opinion about a region reveals the inhibiting factors, it cannot convey the comparative strength of these factors in a manner which will be a tool for the administrator. Stating that the average audience of area x is extremely sensitive about criticism, warns the administrator of a diffuse character trait in his region, but the term "extremely" does not add an important datum to his awareness. Another author, writing about the same region, may use "extremely" to denote his own perception of intensity which may or may not coincide with the previous author's. There is no semantic standardization of adjectives of degree. A British enthnologist's "rather" may have just about the same meaning as a young American anthropologist's "extremely."

Next arises the thorny question of what to do when administrative expedience conflicts with cultural tradition. The question becomes complicated by the fact that the alien administrator generally subscribes to a set of moral values different from indigenous values. As pointed out above, the Westerner might well consider the Indian practice of using or manipulating the Scriptures as unethical. It would probably be unethical for an administrator to attempt to impose his values on his audience or to adopt values inconsistent with his own. The anthropologist cannot say whether operational considerations should overrule ethical reflections, for this is a philosophical decision. He can point out the dilemma and suggest cultural variants affecting solutions. He is neither a moralist nor the administrator; the moralist may volunteer counsel, especially when he is not charged with making decisions. The anthropologist's task is to predict cultural reaction to administrative procedure, but the administrator is not bound by such prediction.

In most cases the administrator can reach a satisfactory solution through candid discussion with his audience. The administrator should be able to divert attention from most potential blocks. If no one raises objections, the administrator should go ahead with his business. Respect for local peculiarities which might interest the philosopher, archaeologist, or anthropologist does not justify hesitation on the part of the administrator. The anthropologist's contribution to the administration of development should be not to create problems but to indicate solutions to existing problems or to facilitate avoidance of potential hurdles.

There is another side to the cultural-hurdle coin. The administrator, himself, often has certain preconceived notions about individual and group attitudes in his assigned area which interfere with a correct evaluation of the cultural situation. It is understandable that the alien administrator, particularly in areas culturally remote from his own, might either fail to recognize cultural hurdles, or "see" hurdles where none exist. But preconceived notions such as "the Irish are . . ." "Indians are . . ." beset the path of the native as well as the alien program administrator.[17] There is a traditional self-image expressed in propositions beginning with "we Irish are . . ." and "we Indians are . . .", and there is a pseudo-scientific alter-image of any alien milieu. A Hindu administrator entrusted with an industrial development task among the Santhals, a large aboriginal group in Bihar, assumes "we Hindus are spiritual people, hence we must go easy in creating an industrial pattern." His assumption derives from the highly eclectic modern Hindu self-image, which is based on nostalgia rather than fact.[18] This self-image is reinforced by the popular occidental image of India. But it so happens that the Santhals are not at all spiritual in any sense this particular administrator assumes. An extrovert, sensuous personality structure is considerably more common among the Santhals than among surrounding caste-Hindu groups.[19]

The objection that everyone knows it is harmful to entertain preconceived notions and prejudices is too general to be helpful. Preconceived ethnic notions are highly specific biases, and it requires directed effort and the sort of study suggested earlier to dispel such preconceptions. Before the administrator takes up his work, he must acquaint himself with the general cultural patterns of the society in which he will serve, be that his own or a totally alien one.

We have been discussing situations which are specific in terms of area and culture. At least one general principle emerges from our propositions. This general principle might be called "multiple configuration expectancy"; "expectancy" is "multiple" because the administrator and his audience belong to the same or to different social milieu. The multiple configuration expectancy principle appears in four patterns:

(a) the cultural self-image of the audience to which the development program is administered;

(b) the cultural self-image of the administrators;

(c) the alter-image of the audience, i.e., the image which the audience thinks the administrator has of its members;

(d) the alter-image of the administrator, i.e., the image the administrator thinks the audience has of him.

An Indian illustration of this general principle can be depicted:

(a) we, members of the *panchāyat,* are experienced, traditionally and pragmatically educated, sagacious leaders of the community;

(b) I, Mr. Banerji, ICS, am a Hindu by birth, a British administrator by training, attached to my own traditions, but intellectually committed to the values taught by such British thinkers as Tennyson, T. S. Eliot, and Harold Laski;

(c) that bookish, city-dwelling, trouser-wearing Bengali Brahmin *bābū* thinks of us as good, simple, uneducated folks, who must be coaxed into what he thinks or says is good for us;

(d) these *panchāyat* men are shrewd in their own way; they know our weakness and they may doubt the sincerity of the administration. They know that I am learned, but they think I am unpractical, peevish, etc.

Consideration of an area in the patterns of multiple configuration expectancy gives an awareness of the interplay and interrelationships between the administrator and his audience. By constant reassessment of his acquired knowledge in terms of actual field experience and a flexible adaptation of the demands of modernization to those of tradition, the administrator can fashion his methods of introducing change to yield positive results.

What are, in fine, the implications of this study for the civil servant, particularly on the administrative and executive level? The anthropologist would love to advise the administrator to study cultural anthropology and cultural hurdles; but then the sociologist would suggest that the administrator do the same with sociology, the psychologist with psychology. Clearly, such suggestions are not operational, but there are a few minimal points, rules of thumb, which can be derived profitably from this survey.

In order to create an awareness of possible cultural hurdles, the administrator should consider his area in the framework of the multiple configuration expectancy. He should be aware that cultural hurdles are mutual, that both he and the audience supply them, and that there is no such thing as one-sided cultural mischief.

He should listen with particular attention to sophisticated or learned opinion about his audience. He must strive to distinguish cultural hurdles, conditioned by peculiarities in his area's tradition, from what we have called universal psychological hurdles, e.g., fear, general poverty, insecurity, ignorance. Changes which are objectively incompatible with tradition must be distinguished from those that are only believed incompatible. Obstacles arising from cultural as distinguished from universal hurdles can often be circumvented by reference to tradition. Only by such understandings can the administrator's methods be designed to minimize friction between modernization and tradition.

Finally, failure to introduce innovation because of real or fancied cultural hurdles is the worst sort of procedure. We have noted that the administrator is not a moralist or philosopher: his job is to get things done. It is far better to act, taking actual or potential hurdles into account and adjusting to specific situations, than to dismiss desired change because it appears "culturally impossible."

NOTES

1. See my "Saffron Robes and *Joie de Vivre*—a letter from Thailand," *Quest* (Bombay: 1956).

2. The ruler in Travancore's epithet was the "servant of ViSNu" (God of preservation and wealth—Padmanābhadāsa).

3. The *panchāyat* is the council of five village elders of traditional India. It has been reinstated as the minimum unit of local self-government in independent India. The senior member of this council is at the same time the village headman. A rather good outline of the self-image of the *panchāyat* is given in Ralph H. Retzlaff, *A Case Study of Panchāyats in a North Indian Village* (Berkeley: Center for South Asia Studies, Institute of International Studies, University of California, 1962).

4. Indian Islamic commentaries of the Ahmadīya and Khoja sects and the Muslim mystical tradition have been strongly influenced by Hindu cyclical cosmology.

5. Personal communication from a peasant of Bhojpur. Caste Hindus have their names entered in the records at places of pilgrimage by a *PāNDā*, a Brahmin official at large shrines; this is a meritorious act and the record is of a religious deed.

6. A skit presented for the students of Pilani University in Rajasthan in 1951 demonstrates such universal hurdles. In it a trouser-wearing administrator tries to persuade a villager to use a project's new methods of irrigation. The villager listens attentively and even lauds the project, but constantly reverts to the *cilkhā,* an ancient water-splashing device, and refuses

to see that the new scheme would make the *cilkhā* redundant. The older contraption comes up repeatedly in the villager's refrain. The villager finally convinces the weary administrator that while his project is more efficient, the *cilkhā* is more reliable and gives the farmer stronger muscles. This skit is representative. The villager will not adduce such quasi-sophisticated reasons for retaining his old equipment as manual labor is better for man's morality or the host of moralizing propositions which the Indian nationalist movement has brought in its wake. Nor does the villager seem to feel that the simpler devices are in any way nobler. The villager's initial objections may be stubborn and archaic but their do not stem from traditional attitudes peculiar to his culture.

7. Even in India or Pakistan, there does not seem to be much of the exasperating attitude that "my father and his father did x in fashion y; hence y and x are good enough for me." Fears of such attitudes do not seem based on much field observation but on pre-anthropological notions of the "wise, stubborn man of the land."

8. Knowledge of such canonically supported, popular ideas will benefit administrators in non-Indian areas where there is a large Hindu audience, e.g., East Africa, the Fiji Islands, British Guiana, and East Pakistan.

9. *Mahārishi Vālmīki*, produced Bombay in 1947; *Jhanak Jhanak Pa'il bāje*, Bombay, 1955; *Jhānsī kī Rānī*, Bombay, 1953; *Rām Rājya*, Bombay, 1944 (this is a popular representation of the epic *RāmāyaNa*, and was the only movie Mr. Gandhi ever saw and recommended); and *Baijū BāwRā*.

10. Personal communication from the late M. N. Roy, leader of Communist party, 1952.

11. See W. Norman Brown, "The Content of Cultural Continuity in India," *Journal of Asian Studies*, XXIV, 1961; also Milton Singer, "Cultural Values in India's Economic Development," *Annals of the American Academy of Political and Social Sciences*, CCCV, May, 1956. These two authors advance the thesis that Hindu tradition poses few barriers to innovation.

12. Personal communication (New Delhi, 1955).

13. Personal communication from the late M. N. Roy (Dahra Doon, India, August, 1951).

14. See the *Bhagavadgītā*, 2nd Canto, "*hato vā prāpsyase svargam jitvā tu bhoKSase mahīm . . .*" ("if you are killed, you will go to heaven, if you win, you will enjoy the earth . . ." hence fight, kill your relatives and other kinsmen.) The *Bhagavadgītā* is the most important of moral codes in modern Hinduism, and almost all leaders have interpreted this book according to their light and for their purposes.

15. This is a caveat for academicians as well. Very often, a person is invited to a highly specialized Orientalist scholar's talk because "he was in India two years ago" (on a world tour, en route to elsewhere on business, etc.). Nor does an Indian student of chemical engineering know more about India than an Amercian chemical engineer knows about America.

16. Clerks and white collar workers of all kinds, short of executives, are

called "bābū" all over India. The term was first used in Bengal, the home of the first British-Indian administrative units.

17. A logician might call this phenomenon a "subjective counterfactual" or subjective hurdle pattern.

18. For an excellent analysis of this problem, see E. Shils, *The Intellectual between Tradition and Modernity: The Indian Situation* ("Series Comparative Studies in Society and History," Supplement No. 1 [The Hague, Mouton & Co., 1961]).

19. See N. Datta-Majumder, *The Santal—a Study in Culture Change* (Memoir No. 2, published by the Department of Anthropology, Government of India, New Delhi: 1956); also M. Orans, "A Tribal People in an Industrial Setting," in Milton Singer, ed., *Traditional India; Structure and Change* ("Bibliographical Series," Vol. X [Philadelphia: American Folklore Society, 1959]).

V

Motivation for Change and Development Administration

PAUL MEADOWS

"Perhaps the most difficult thing for planners—and students as well—to fit into their frames of reference is that what peoples under tutelage learn from their tutors is continuously being projected against their own pre-existing cultural background; that however simple a technology and an economic order may be, they exist as hard psycho-cultural facts; that no people present a historical *tabula rasa* on which the planner from outside may write as he will."[1]

"Whether the item of culture is ready to change or not depends upon its meaning within the group concerned. And similarly whether an item of culture coming from outside will be effective in initiating change or not depends upon whether it carries a sufficient amount of the right sort of meaning."[2]

THE MOTIVATIONAL APPROACH TO THE PROBLEM OF CHANGE

Since the end of World War II, concern with economic and social development has been characterized by a behavior-oriented view of society. Sigmund Neumann suggests that the twentieth century has witnessed three stages in approach to development.[3] Prior to World War I rationalist idealists, envisioning the spread of democratic institutions and inter-people harmony, stressed constitutional and administrative structures. With what seemed an irrational collapse of collective security in the interwar years, naive utopianism was replaced by equally naive cynicism, suspicious of panaceas and interested only in material forces for engineering development. Neumann characterizes the present behavioral approach as "realism with vision."

In a developing society it is, after all, the people who develop. Some are administrators, some participants; all must consciously or unconsciously accept or reject change. All development indices, goals, and agencies center on the experiences of human beings. In the final analysis, the development process turns on the question of what people value for themselves.

Development administration can be regarded as the public management of economic and social change in terms of deliberate public policy. The development administrator is concerned with guiding change. J. H. Adler has observed that in comparison with the development process in underdeveloped countries, growth in developed nations "is smooth, predictable and 'rational'."[4] What seems to the Western observer as irrational and unpredictable, may, in reality however, often be a reflection of lack of understanding of the culture and motivations of the underdeveloped society. The theme of this paper is that successful development administration depends upon knowledge and utilization of those factors and processes which motivate change. Some of these processes might well be "irrational"; if so, the way to induce acceptance of change may be to appeal to the irrational.

Social theorists have long searched for a general theory of change. The cause, function, and logic in the process of change have been conceptualized in apocalyptic, utopian, evolutionary, cyclic, spiral, or devolutionary patterns of change. The very proliferation of such theories tends to confirm sociologist Talcott Parsons' observations:

> A general theory of the processes of change of social systems is not possible in the present state of knowledge. The reason is very simply that such a theory would imply complete knowledge of the laws of process of the system and this knowledge we do not possess.[5]

We do not propose to propound another theory of change but rather to demonstrate that the tools and approach of motivational theory can greatly facilitate the development administrator's task of inducing cooperation in the innovative process. The type of change demanded by development is not merely increase in size or shift in the income structure or resource-institution pattern of a society. Development by definition requires alterations in customary behavior patterns. The climate of development is a climate of innovation, modification, and alteration of personal attitudes, organizational practices, and institutions. Development administration, because it is prompted by the urgencies and dimensions of total change, is perhaps the most revolutionary of all the major transformations changing the face and form of societies the world over. Here we are concerned with the small, but utterly significant area of development—the problem of motivation.

All motivational theory stresses the variability of meaning in human experience, for the variability of meaning is the very matrix of change. People will define the meaning of a situation differently, they will come up with different evaluations, they will derive or impute different norms, and certainly they will feel about the situation in many, many different ways and intensities. No development administrator can afford to neglect these dimensions of response. Obviously one cannot motivate a man to act by appealing in terms outside his comprehesion; words or symbols of appeal must be understandable and make sense to the individual. Equally important is the point made by C. Wright Mills:

> Motives are of no value apart from delimited societal situations for which they are appropriate vocabularies. They must be situated. . . . Motives vary in content and character with historical epochs and societal structures.[6]

Motives will also vary for the individual depending upon the measuring rod or standard by which he is gauging his behavior. As Max Weber noted in connection with work, "The motives which induce people to work vary with different social classes. . . . When a man changes rank, he switches from one set of motives to another."[7]

Social scientists are fond of saying that we learn our motives, at least we learn certain essential aspects of them. We learn what responses should be made, where and when, in what manner or style, with what goals and norms, and with what meanings to ourselves and others. Motives are drawn from, and constantly relate to, a store of experiences which is commonly called "culture." From such a store society learns what and how to *see* (the cognitive dimension of motivation), what and how to *feel* (the emotional dimension of motivation), and what and how to *judge* (the normative and evaluative dimension of motivation).

Since motives are socially derived and shaped, motivation can thus most fruitfully be studied in a social context. At the same time, motives tend to achieve functional autonomy; historically people's attitudes have altered long before their organizational or institutional environment has changed. In the next section of this paper we discuss the concept of reference groups as the social contexts of motivation in managed change. While not of direct operational significance to the administrator, the approach and perspective of reference group analysis should greatly facilitate the innovator's task of persuading tradition-bound societies to accept change.

Reference Groups and Motivational Theory

Every society's culture is a storehouse of semiotic or symbolic structures which function as "the more or less organized systems of meaning by which a thinking man gauges the historical situation and adopts a role with relation to it."[8] For the purposes of operational analysis such structures or systems of meaning may be described as *reference orientations.* Individuals sharing or identifying with similar reference orientations are related to one another in *reference groups.* The concept of reference groups with which individuals either are or aspire to be identified has been developed and elaborated as a tool of social analysis by Robert K. Merton.[9] For our purposes it is sufficient to note that reference groups and reference orientations serve three major functions; they are devices for assessing behavior, gauges of status, and objects of aspiring identification. The lower echelon public administrator, for example, gauges his own and other's activity by the top administrators' patterns of behavior, measures prestige and influence according to these patterns, and uses them as targets for his own aspiring. Reference orientations serve as models and media for definition and action—challenging, inhibiting, inducing, directing or reinforcing behavior. Variously formed and expressed, they have common characteristics. They contain general evaluative elements, and relate to the various roles which people play in society. They are especially important to people when new roles in new settings are being demanded or when conflicts in roles and norms in different contexts must be resolved.

Individuals differ in their capacity to internalize and intellectualize their reference orientations and in the desire to explain or rationalize reference orientations. Some individuals see sharp dichotomies between good and evil, superior and inferior, ours and theirs. Others are ambiguous and manipulate reference orientations in vague political oration.

Reference orientations and groups, whether as roles or belief systems, institutions or clusters of sentiment, pattern human behavior around norms or modes of collective expectations. These reference groups provide the focus of our general approach to the problem of motivation in relation to development administration. It is in these reference groups that the development administrator can discover what Herskovits calls the "hard psycho-cultural facts" of the indigenous society. We shall suggest that the development administrator approach the problem of directed change by understanding the source of change and seek to secure the appropriate response by managing motivation. The administrator would actually become involved in referencing behavior, in encouraging reference orientations which identify with the means and ends of change.

The Case of Japan

In the West and in developing countries elsewhere the intellectuals play a strategic part in the modernization process. The alternatives confronting intellectuals in describing and promoting modernization will, of course, vary from culture to culture. The alternatives confronting the Japanese intellectuals have been outlined in a very perceptive study by two well-known specialists on Japan, J. W. Bennett and R. K. McKnight.[10] Their discussion serves to clarify the relation of reference groups—in this case the Japanese intellectuals—to the processes of directed social change. What they describe as conservative, liberal, and pragmatic hypotheses, three "firmly explicit and public orientations," are, in terms of this analysis, reference orientations. These reference orientations have responded quite differently to the demands of change.

People with financial means and political authority interested in Japan's glory and power have generally urged the conservative orientation, asserting "that the successful modernization of Japan was dependent upon maximal continuity with Japanese cultural tradition." However when confronted with the need to accept more than just Western technology, the conservatives have generally accommodated themselves to cultural changes.

The liberal orientation, urging adoption of Western models of social development and indiscriminate borrowing from the West, has not been popular since the 1890's. Faced with problems of cultural relevance, the liberals have become pragmatic, interested in suggesting parallels between Western and Japanese culture.

The pragmatic orientation stresses resolution of specific situational problems arguing that "more global attitudes and long-term platforms of change which derived from systematic cultural models were inadequate to meet the complex needs of modern Japanese civilization." Noting a trend toward the pragmatic synthesis rather than any single cultural model, Bennett and McKnight observe:

> More generally, the whole conservative platform of modernization contributed to the growth of a cultural medium in which people—especially the highly educated—could assume purposes counter to the conservative goals, generally in the direction of pro-Western liberalism. In turn, these proponents of liberal reforms contributed to cultural change through their own innovations: translations of Western books; their own writings and teachings; and, in some periods, direct political action.[11]

Bennett and McKnight give other insights which could well prove useful to the modernizer in Japan. Japanese intellectuals have generally not demonstrated the emotional detachment in regard to innovation or freedom in national or cultural identification common among intellectuals in the West. They were struck by "the durability of the cultural base and the ability of conservative leaders to make cultural ends compatible with a variety of new techniques, ideas, and world views." Their study makes it clear that the dynamic of change can only be understood in terms of the references and motivations in relation to which people are changing.

Thus both the impact of specific innovations and the ideological or political motivations of the innovators contribute to an explanation of the dynamics of cultural and technical change in a complex society.

Economic History and Motivation Theory

The economist as historian or as practitioner has also, wittingly or unwittingly, used the motivational and reference group approach in theorizing about change.[12] J. Boeke, a major exponent of the school of economic dualism which focuses on the differences in psychology and social organization between Westerners or Western-oriented individuals and societies and Traditional societies. According to Boeke, in locating what factors determine response to economic stimuli in Traditional societies, the practitioner must make a detailed study of the Traditionals. Only then can he construct "a parallel system of economic theory relevant to the special psychological orientations of the traditional community in which he is interested."

A Weberian or comparative approach is used in varied forms by many contemporary students of economic growth. This approach involves comparison of capitalist and socialist societies with special attention to the preconditions of development in each. The student then constructs a model of the socio-psychological constants which are both necessary and sufficient for economic development.

There is a third or monistic approach, used by some exponents of various schools—Classical, Neo-classical, Marxian, and Institutionalist. The names Bagehot, Myrdal, and Hoselitz come to mind. This approach assumes that all peoples have the same basic psychological drives and capacities for development. The traditional economies have been slow to develop because of specific barriers which are rooted in natural factors or in prevailing social and economic structures. The practitioner must assess those barriers and determine strategies for their modification.

These economic interpretations and modes of analysis are actually varieties of motivational theory. The means which the different theories suggest for promoting development are aspects of motivational strategy. The dualist school approach is very similar to that presently followed by international aid agencies. These agencies direct efforts toward identifying basic factors which determine the nature of response to economic stimuli in the various underdeveloped countries. The agencies then construct systems of action designed to evoke the appropriate responses in each particular case. Sometimes such efforts are

linked to statements concerning the nature of motivation. Such
efforts are obviously based on assumption, for basic determinants
cannot scientifically be identified. The strategy suggested by the
second or comparative school of economic thought has unfortunately relied too heavily on examples of development in the
West. Also few general preconditions of development have been
or could be tested. The monistic school faces that tentacular
opponent known as cultural variability. However, it can with
cogency point to generalized barriers to development, and the
assertion that development will follow the removal of such
restraints is indeed testable.

An Analytical Model

Reference orientations and groups are particularly important
tools of motivational theory in analyzing the processes of
managed change. An invaluable study of global modernization,
Industrialism and Industrial Man, by Clark Kerr and associates,
observes that:

> Each industrializing system becomes a 'way of life,' no matter
> what its specific form, and a 'way of life' demands internal
> acceptance and external protection if it is to function success-
> fully in the long run.[13]

Deliberate change, the study maintains, is the work of a minority or elite group. Five such groups are identified: dynastic elite,
middle class, revolutionary intellectuals, colonial administrators,
and nationalist leaders. "Each of these elite groups has a strategy
by which it seeks to order the surrounding society in a consistent
and compatible fashion."[14] Kerr and his associates note the
following goal expectations of the different leadership groups.
Dynastic elites wish to preserve the old order, paternalistically
maintaining authority over the new methods of production. This
goal requires a reasonably strong state which insists on internal
stability. In the work sectors, managers must copy the dynastic
elite's paternalism and workers must remain dependent and
loyal. The *middle class elites,* seeking the greatest welfare of the
individual, turn to the open market, emphasize private initiative, "a pluralistic distribution of rule-making authority," and
self-interest motivation. The *revolutionary intellectuals* project a
new social organization to conform with modern technology: a

powerful state, centralizing rule-making authority and exploiting the citizens' "social-interest" motivation, which prompts acceptance of authority in the interest of public welfare. The *nationalist leaders* desire the independence and progress of the nation under the aegis of the state.

The dynastic elite offers continuity; the middle class, individual choice; the revolutionary intellectuals, high velocity industrialization; the nationalist leaders, the integrity and advancement of the nation.[15]

The differences in approach to modernization can be illustrated by the groups' attitudes toward three problem areas:[16]

A. Pace of Modernization

Dynastic: "No faster than necessary to preserve the traditional elite and its values. Military needs may dictate a more rapid pace."

Middle Class: "Pace set by prospects of private gain, individual choices and limited actions of government. Moderate pace."

Revolutionary Intellectuals: "The fastest possible pace under an extensive set of controls."

Colonial Administrators: "Dependent solely upon the advantage of the mother country."

Nationalist Leaders: "High aspiration and promises but uncertain rate."

B. Priorities in Development

Dynastic: "Preserve and protect agriculture; public works, monuments and paternalistic projects including housing."

Middle Class: "Agriculture compressed by international competition. Sequence depends on market and traditional pattern is from consumers to basic industry. Housing depends on market."

Revolutionary Intellectuals: "Agriculture compressed by draining manpower and preventing individual agriculture enterprises. Priority to basic industry with a vengeance. Housing compressed."

Colonial Administrators: "Industries developed which furnish materials or consumption goods to mother country or supply foreign exchange."

Nationalist Leaders: "Aspires to a broad industrial base, expands on the range of the previous colonial administrator. Prestige items."

C. Access to Management

Dynastic: "Access based upon the family with professionals subordinate to the authority of the family."

Middle Class: "Access to management on basis of initiative and competence—early development of professional management."

Revolutionary Intellectuals: "At first, access on basis of political affiliations, later of professional standards."

Colonial Administrators: "Top positions reserved for nationals of the home country."

Nationalist Leaders: "Various, with emphasis on political and professional qualifications."

Acculturation and Cultural Stretch

It should be clear that general "principles" of development administration which ignore the existence of reference groups and the enormous differentials in the political and cultural settings of administered change are hypothetical, if not vacuous and naive. It should be equally clear that there can be no unqualified cross-cultural generalizations about what motivates acceptance or rejection of change in differing societies. The barriers to change will differ, depending upon the motivational context. It is possible to state that while there is cultural limitation on any developmental innovation, there is also a considerable cultural "stretch" through which the novelty can be fit into a receiving culture.

One of the ablest observers of the global modernization process, sociologist W. E. Moore, has considered this cultural "stretch." Moore suggests that "the specific forms of motivation relevant to economic activity are culturally variable and to be adequately understood only within particular institutional contexts."[17] However, "the industrially utilizable incentives are not so narrow as commonly conceived in traditional theory, and may therefore be assumed to be somewhat adaptable cultural systems."[18] It is possible to generalize with respect to the emergence of new reference orientations and motives on the basis of observation of contacts between cultures. We shall here merely summarize Moore's generalizations:[19]

1. The greater the number of lines of contact with an external culture, the greater is the force of the new influence.

2. Acceptance is much greater and easier if contact with the new element is continuous and, in principle, permanent.

3. Under equivalent conditions simple elements are more readily transferable than complex ones, simple cultural forms more than complex cultural meanings.

4. The more unsuitable the existing circumstances, the more necessary it will be to rely on slow fermentation or for leaders to sponsor change by "hothouse" development, as in Japan.

5. Acceptance is greater and easier if innovation coincides with the sense of advantage of those with vested interests.

6. The higher the prestige level of the innovators, the faster the rate of acceptance.

7. The "greater the dissimilarity of cultures, or the more unsuitable the prevailing social and psychological attributes for the new development, the more difficult the transition and the greater the change necessary in the alien system if the transfer is actually completed."

8. The rate and areas of acceptance are a function of the intensity and direction of expectation of change.

9. Acceptance varies with the tension level, or gratification level, characterizing relations between external and internal cultures.

These generalizations suggest approaches or strategies for the development administrator seeking to manage meaningfulness and motivate individual acceptance of change. Resistance can be converted into compliance as threats are transformed into promise, risk into security, liabilities into assets. As F. C. Bartlett noted as early as 1943:

Every culture has its "hard" and its "soft" points. If change is sought at the former, it will provide resistance and very likely open discord; while the latter are yielding and it is from them that reformation will spread.[20]

The acculturative contexts of change, now rapidly appearing the world over, are motivational resources for change. And fundamentally, development administration everywhere offers one outstanding rhetorical appeal—that of modernity.

Some Strategies of Motivational Appeal

The concept of what constitutes modernity has undergone vast changes as it has moved out of the salons and libraries of the intellectuals. Daniel Lerner, in a fascinating study of the Middle East, notes that in the nineteenth and first half of the twentieth century modernization meant Europeanization of the upper or leisure class.[21] Modernization in the contemporary world is different in at least two respects. First, it does not mean Europeanization or wholesale copying of the West. The emerging nations do not wish to be like the West but to be modern as the West is modern: to modernize is not necessarily to Westernize. Each nation is seeking to achieve its own pattern of modernity. Another significant aspect of contemporary modernization is that it is diffused throughout society and, as Lerner notes, "touches public institutions as well as private aspirations."

Lerner describes the traditional society as essentially non-participant:

> It deploys people by kinship into communities isolated from each other and from a center; without an urban-rural division of labor, it develops new needs requiring economic interdependence; lacking the bonds of interdependence, people's horizons are limited by locale and their decisions involve only other *known* people in *known* situations. Hence, there is no need for a transpersonal common doctrine formulated in terms of shared secondary symbols—a national 'ideology' which enables persons unknown to each other to engage in political controversy to achieve 'consensus' by comparing their opinion. Modern society is participant in that it functions by 'consensus'—individuals making personal decisions on public issues must concur with other individuals they do not know to make possible a stable common governance.[22]

J. S. Coleman in an impressive summary of a wide variety of developing political cultures also identifies participation as an essential aspect of modern society. He calls attention to the "wide gap which exists between the traditional mass and the essentially modern sub-society of the Westernized elite."[23] The latter control the central government apparatus, seeking to speak for the entire society. They are in fact the main focus of political activity and change in the society.

Perhaps the most notable fact about the seventy-six countries treated in the Almond-Coleman survey is "the fragmented character of their political cultures." Coleman describes two basic types of internal cleavage which severely handicap any attempt at development or modernization in the emerging nation. There is a gap between the urban, modern subsociety of the Westernized elements and the traditional societies, and there is a horizontal cleavage—a "melange of indigenous political cultures which, by the accidents of colonialism, are included within the boundaries of larger territorial political systems."[24]

There seems fairly general agreement on the importance of participation and a high empathic capacity in the development of a modern culture. Lerner defines empathy as "the capacity to see oneself in the other fellow's situation," and high empathic capacity, "the predominant personal style only in modern society," as largely a function of participation. Lerner suggests that

> If modernization is the transition to participant society then the direction of change in public communication is toward a constantly expanding opinion arena. . . . The modernizing tendency is toward networks that can handle maximum participation and concurrently to develop the participants needed to man these networks.[25]

Lerner's suggestions indicate areas in which motivation and reference group theory can have practical importance for the modernizer. The focus is on the importance of mediators in the society which link and interweave parochial segments into closer identification with the center. Development of networks of mass communication is one way of expanding the opinion area. The methods of appeal will be discussed below. Lerner's "participants" could be individuals or reference groups.

S. Eisenstadt's sociological analysis of political development focuses on the individuals and groups which could act as mediators.[26] Eisenstadt proposes that political elites in emerging nations be considered and encouraged as entrepreneurs in fostering political development. Entrepreneurial skills are no less important in the political realm than in the economic. The methods of the political entrepreneur would be vastly different from those of his economic counterpart. His framework is "not that of the impersonal market . . . but that of the more personal elements of political life—struggle over social and community organization."[27]

Eisenstadt suggests that these political entrepreneurs should encourage the development of autonomous social groupings and independent centers of prestige and power within the society. Such mediating groupings could act to raise the level of participation in and empathy with the goals of modernization. The political entrepreneurs would actually be involved in referencing behavior and in fostering reference orientations compatible with a modernizing society. In building a unified political culture the strategic problem, according to Eisenstadt, is to develop "various intervening mechanisms, activities, and mediating institutions which facilitate the establishment of several levels of interlinking spheres within the society."[28]

The Almond-Coleman survey provides extremely valuable insights into the actual operation of theories of political development. J. S. Coleman indicates that governing elites in many emerging nations are seeking to develop just such mediating institutions. They are

> engaged in the development and strengthening of system-wide secondary structures that not only impinge directly upon the individual but also penetrate the primary socializing structures. They are seeking to create, by an act of will, an integrated process of political socialization in which at all levels there is an inculcation of positive sentiments of respect, loyalty and pride in the new politics.[29]

In many cases, however, as Coleman notes,

> Their efforts are being met with strong resistance, especially from particularistic forces—forces which modernization itself ironically tends, in many situations, to strengthen. Moreover,

there are distinct limits to which a political culture can be deliberately created in a single generation. . . .[30]

There are also wide variations in the means of recruiting Eisenstadt's political entrepreneurs—a variety which, according to the Almond-Coleman study, reflects differences in:

(1) the character, and particularly the breadth, of the social bases from which entrants into the political arena are drawn; (2) the circumstances under which, and the avenues through which, members of the society become politically participant; (3) the degree to which the recruitment process is undergoing change; (4) the rate of political activation; and (5) motivations for entering politics.[31]

The experience of the emerging nations in bridging political discontinuities and in creating a unified network of political communication has been conditioned by many factors. Coleman lists several of the more important factors affecting the degree and extent to which local groups identify with the center:

(1) the extent, and particularly the evenness, of the geographical incidence of modernization and social change; (2) the structure of political groups, and particularly the extent to which political organization, recruitment, and participation are national in scope; (3) the linguistic pattern, and particularly the extent to which vernacular languages persist as the main vehicle for communication; and (4) the character and level of development of transportation systems and of the media of mass communication.[32]

We do not propose here to elaborate on either the theoretical or the empirical studies of the emerging nations' experience with managed change. As indicated by the extensive quotations above, proposals for mediating institutions to serve as networks of communication in referencing behavior and the experiences of emerging nations in carrying out such proposals have been competently treated.

Our purpose is rather to suggest the significance of motivational strategies in engrossing human beings in common identifications and goals and to broaden the modernizers' conception of the tools of persuasion that are available. We would suggest that a rationalist-dominated West has yet to sense the universal dynamic which lies untapped in the giant metaphors of human imagination. The West has been preoccupied with rationalist reference orientations and the accounting austerities of capitalist economics. There is a vast reservoir of motivational resources which center not in logic but in imagination, not in syllogism but in mythology, not in the formal but in the semiotic structures. This theme has been developed by a variety of modern writers.[33]

Development administration is an act of imagination which attracts, fires, holds, and elaborates the loyalties of human beings engaged in goal-directed change. This involvement is less through words than through images which bind together the real and the ideal, the fact and the hope, the hate and the love, the present and the future, the rational and the nonrational, the organizational and the personal. The image joins the object symbol and the metaphor, the thing and its comparison. The image thus embodies resistance and the change which it proclaims.

The management of meaningful imagination—of meaningful image-formation and of image-projection—requires that each political culture seek out its own persuasive projections of reality. For the metaphors of political imagination are meaningful chiefly in the context of the given culture experience. If the clue to modernization is participation, then the clue to participation lies in an imagery which embodies the traditions of the past with an emerging tradition of change. This imagery, culture-bound in character, is also culture-transcending. The metaphorical unity which subsocieties within cultures can share with one another, which cultures can share with other cultures, must be sought in myth, as Georges Sorel observed many years ago. The idea-in-the-image, the image-in-the-idea—herein lie the creative and persuasive potentials of managed change.

Development administration must rely less on motivational strategies which appeal to the construction of clear and attractive cognitive structures. Such "rational" models assume that motivation and behavior are structured according to rational fact. More persuasive is the relatively unknown landscape in which the intuitive is the mode of learning and the image is the vehicle of projection. It is a countryside in which the metaphors of imagination are the cement that binds dissident fragments of political cultures in an integration of meanings which are so savagely splintered in a world undergoing rapid and intense, but creative, emergence.

NOTES

1. F. C. Bartlett, "Psychological Methods for the Study of 'Hard' or 'Soft' Features of Culture," *Africa*, XVI (1946), 147-48.

2. Melville Herskovits, "African Economic Development in Cross-Cultural Perspective," *American Economics Association Papers and Proceedings*, XLVI (1956), 459.

3. Sigmund Neumann, "Comparative Politics: A Half-Century Appraisal," *Journal of Politics*, XIX (1957), 369ff.

4. J. H. Adler, "Some Policy Problems in Economic Development," *Economic Development and Cultural Change*, IX (1961), 113.

5. Talcott Parsons, *The Social System* (Glencoe: The Free Press, 1951), p. 486.

6. C. W. Mills, "Situated Actions and Vocabularies of Motive," *American Sociological Review*, V (1940), 913.

7. Paraphrased by K. Mannheim in *Ideology and Utopia* (Harcourt, Brace, 1936), pp. 316-17.

8. Kenneth Burke, *Attitudes toward History*, vol. II (New York: New Republic, Inc., 1937), pp. 1-2. (In reference to semiology, a science pertaining to signs and in medicine to symptoms, we stress the deep-seated aspects of motives as well as the verbalized and formulated aspects.)

9. See Robert K. Merton, *Social Theory and Social Structure* (Glencoe: The Free Press, 1957), pp. 225-386.

10. J. W. Bennett and R. K. McKnight, "Approaches of the Japanese Innovator to Cultural and Technical Change," *Annals of the American Academy*, CCCV (May, 1956).

11. *Ibid.*, p. 133.

12. The following treatment is taken from T. W. Shea, Jr., "Theoretical Problems of Economic Growth," *Journal of Economic History*, Suppl. VII (1947).

13. C. Kerr, J. T. Dunlop, I. H. Harbison, C. A. Myers, *Industrialism and Industrial Man* (Cambridge: Harvard University Press, 1960), p. 51.

14. *Ibid.*, p. 50.

15. *Ibid.*, pp. 75-76.

16. *Ibid.*, p. 98.

17. W. E. Moore, *Industrialization and Labor, Social Aspects of Economic Development* (Ithaca: Cornell University Press, 1951), p. 178.

18. *Ibid.*
19. *Ibid.*, pp. 179-198.
20. F. C. Bartlett, *op. cit.*, pp. 147-48.
21. Daniel Lerner, *The Passing of the Traditional Society* (Glencoe: The Free Press, 1958).
22. *Ibid.*, p. 50.
23. G. A. Almond and J. S. Coleman (eds.), *The Politics of Developing Areas* (Princeton: Princeton University Press, 1960), pp. 535-36.
24. *Ibid.*, p. 545.
25. Lerner, *op. cit.*, p. 69.
26. S. Eisenstadt, "Sociological Aspects of Political Development in Underdeveloped Countries," in S. N. Lipset and N. J. Smelser (eds.), *Sociology: The Progress of a Decade* (New York: Prentice-Hall, 1961).
27. *Ibid.*
28. *Ibid.*
29. Almond and Coleman, *op. cit.*, p. 545.
30. *Ibid.*
31. *Ibid.*, p. 546.
32. *Ibid.*, p. 557.
33. See for example: Jean-Paul Sartre, *Psychology of the Imagination* (New York: Philosophical Library, 1948); Kenneth Boulding, *The Image* (Ann Arbor: University of Michigan Press, 1956); Martin Foss, *Symbol and Metaphor in Human Experience* (Princeton: Princeton University Press, 1949); H. F. Simon, *Revolution, Whither Bound?* (New York: Farrar and Rinehart, 1935).

VI

Economics as Part of Development Administration

IRVING SWERDLOW

THE TITLE of this essay is designed to emphasize, even at some cost to brevity, what is often overlooked—that economic growth is only part of the complex social, political, psychological, cultural, and economic process called "development" or, more recently, "modernization."[1] This process, involving changes in nearly every important inter-personal and inter-group relationship within a society, is probably the most complicated subject man has attempted to study and understand. So far, it is likely that not even the main variables of the process have been identified, and the study of most functional relationships is still at a relatively primitive fact-finding stage.

The facts, theories, suppositions, and myths concerning social organization that have been accumulated from centuries of study have been grouped into ill-defined, heterogeneous categories called "disciplines," each of which tends to view the modernization process through its own vocabulary, concepts, and analytical tools. Serious students in any one of these disciplines would readily admit that theirs can only be a partial view of the total modernization process, and that the total analysis is far more complex than mere addition of partial analyses. This essay assumes that there is not now, and in all likelihood cannot be, a single, comprehensive theory that satisfactorily explains the causal relationships among even the major variables in the modernization process.

This essay discusses (1) why there is a confusion between economic growth and the total process of modernization, (2) why public administrators in underdeveloped countries become so deeply involved in economic activities, and (3) some important economic relationships that are often overlooked or misunderstood by public administrators. This essay hopes to demonstrate that the attitudes and decisions of public administrators are so important to economic growth that improving their understanding of basic economic relationships is of vital importance to development administration.

Economic Growth and Modernization

Two mis-identities are apparently widely held: modernization is identified with economic growth and economic growth is identified as depending solely on economic activities. Clearly, both are wrong, though it is understandable why the mistakes are made. Most people in countries with a low standard of living really mean economic development when they speak of a "developed" status for their country. In general, they mean a higher standard of living, and they usually recognize that this requires increased production by using better methods to produce and distribute their goods and services. What they fail to recognize is that this is only part of the modernization process—and only part of the end result; a part that cannot, in the twentieth century, be abstracted from the political, social, cultural, and psychological matrix which is the totality of their society.

These mis-identities are not limited to the uneducated masses. They are often held by the educated elite including many, if not most, public administrators. It is a rare public administrator indeed who firmly perceives the implications of modernization for the political structure of his country. Unfortunately, the most perceptive are often the few who dominate in many underdeveloped countries and who resist modernization because they realize it means a deterioration of their prestige and power. Giving lip service to modernization, these elites consciously and unconsciously fight to retain their position by making the process of modernization more difficult.

It is not surprising, therefore, that economic growth becomes the core about which other kinds of changes are grouped, the tent which covers such changes. Modernization is presented largely in economic terms—higher standards of living, more goods and services, better housing, more employment, more efficient and comfortable production methods. Per capita GNP, a narrow and technically limited concept, is seen as an accurate index of modernization.

Comprehensive economic plans are both a result and a cause

of such narrow conceptions. They are couched largely in economic terms on the assumption that economic matters are far easier to control and manipulate than other aspects of modernization. It is also assumed that many sociological and political obstacles to progress will disappear when economic obstacles are removed. Plans usually affect the social and political life of the community with proposals for cooperatives, public banking institutions, new roads, schools, and similar change-making developments. But the political and social effects of such proposals are only vaguely identified; it may be self-defeating to be too explicit. Rarely are cultural and psychological effects mentioned in plans because to advocate such changes might be considered antinational. In any case, so little is known of the causes, results, and relationships of these noneconomic changes that not much could be planned. The planning process, to which nearly all underdeveloped countries are fanatically devoted, therefore provides a substantial means for emphasizing economic growth to the near exclusion of all other aspects of modernization.

Public administrators have special reason for accepting this overemphasis on economic growth and economic activities. In most of these countries, government has always played an important role in the production and distribution of goods and services. Government participation has generally not been limited to the formation of broad policies, to the creation of a favorable "business climate," or to the arbitration of disputes. Participation usually involved direct control over large quantities of the factors of production, through control over individual transactions, through ownership or licensing or marketing arrangements. Where large foreign private investment was concerned, the line dividing private and public officials was paper thin or nonexistent from the viewpoint of a colony's native inhabitants. Even where Marxist or socialist ideologies are not widely accepted, government's major role in economic affairs is as firmly accepted as is the predominance of free enterprise in our system.

A quotation that refers to Indonesia, but applies to most underdeveloped countries, summarizes this point well:

Revolutionary nationalism has endowed the state with an

almost charismatic character, with which the younger generation in particular has identified all its inspirations. In consequence, the improvement of individual or mass is seen as a state function; hence the intense, idealistic interest of even the very young in politics. Independent of the omnipotent all regulating state, welfare and progress are held to be difficult, if not impossible, to achieve.[2]

Most administrators, at least at the upper levels, are sufficiently sophisticated to recognize that noneconomic changes are involved. They regard these changes, however, as dependent variables which cannot or should not be deliberately influenced by government officials and, therefore, are not important to their own functions. The usual glib clichés about changes in all phases of community life are quite superficial and rarely represent real convictions that influence administrative operations. Moreover, it is usually risky or considered bad taste for a public servant to talk about necessary changes in social and psychological terms since such areas are considered beyond his competence and duty.[3]

Administration and Economics

It is much easier to explain why administrators in underdeveloped countries identify economic growth with the entire modernizing process than it is to outline the administrator's relationship to economic growth. For, as asserted above, government is significantly involved in nearly every type of economic activity. And government is only people acting and influencing others under powers given or attributed to them as government officials.

When a government seeks to implement rapid economic growth as a country's major goal, all key officials "get into the act" consciously or unconsciously. Not that they must serve as professional economists. This can be left, albeit unsuccessfully thus far, to specialists in such agencies as the Central Bank, Ministry of Finance, or Budget Office, whose assignments require some technical knowledge of economics. A United Nations study summarized this point very aptly: "Economic programs depend to a large extent upon the adoption by governments of appropriate administrative and legislative actions, both in the public and the private sectors."[4]

Even a hasty examination in an underdeveloped country seriously attempting modernization would confirm this generalization. If a major metropolitan area were observed, one could readily find factories built with government funds and operated by government officials. Quasi-governmental corporations are also becoming common, since corporations are considered modern and therefore efficient. Direct city services, such as schools, hospitals, sewage, and water, would likely be present. There would generally be considerable government building activity, and the major transportation and communication systems would either be government operated or directly licensed with rates set by government. Businessmen would seek and compete for licenses, import permits, and other necessary documents, granted at almost all levels of government—papers varying from police permits for marketing arrangements to government loans for new industries. A large number of men would be consulting government officials on tax matters, regulations for travel abroad, issuance of letters of credit, and information on the availability of government aid. Labor leaders, closely related to government in most underdeveloped countries, would be frequent consultants at all levels of government. Key government officials in the metropolitan area would readily admit that they spend a major part of each day explaining governmental regulations, listening to or reading about appeals from governmental regulations, and, in general, becoming deeply involved in the economic activities of the community.

In a rural area the physical signs of governmental involvement in economic activities may not be as visible as in urban areas, but there is ample evidence that even here most government officials spend a large part of their time managing, controlling, and influencing economic activities. There could be demonstration and seed farms directly operated by government. Government sale of fertilizer and seed is becoming common, while often government purchasing agencies are established to dominate the market for cash crops for export. Government "extension" workers and "village aid" workers either exist or are planned in nearly every underdeveloped country.

Government-sponsored cooperatives and agricultural banks are among the earliest and most widespread means adopted to improve agricultural technology.

Having advanced the thesis that economic growth is a particularly important element in the modernization process, and its corollary, that public administrators play a strategic role in economic growth, there remains a third thesis, namely, that public administrators are currently not available in either the quantity or quality required by the emphasis on economic growth.

The inadequacy of public administration in the underdeveloped countries is attested to in the many studies on development which identify adequate administration as an essential precondition to self-sustained economic growth.[5] Ambassador John K. Galbraith, in his widely discussed article in *Foreign Affairs*, considered "a reliable apparatus of government and public administration" so essential to development that he would deny the possibility of economic growth without it.[6] So strategic and relatively scarce is adequate government action that some analysts propose that government should be considered a factor of production in underdeveloped countries, along with capital, labor, and natural resources.[7] The shortage in capacity for making executive decisions, both in the public and private sectors, has led to one of the most challenging recent books on development, which proposes that investment priorities be measured by their effect in increasing executive decision-making capacity.[8]

Plans of underdeveloped countries often call administration a "limiting factor," stress the importance of improved administrative capacity, and in many cases blame failure to achieve Plan goals upon inadequate administration. For example, Pakistan's first Five Year Plan observed that:

> The most serious limitations on the feasibility of the programme are to be found in the area of organization and administration. . . . In a real sense, the first requisite for the success of a development programme at the present time in both the public and private sectors is a substantial reform and improvement in governmental organization and administration.[9]

India's first Five Year Plan states that: "In all directions, the pace of development will depend largely upon the quality of public administration, the efficiency with which it works and the cooperation which it evokes."[10] Ceylon's Plan predicts that inadequate administration may limit development: "The expansion in the public sector provided for by the Plan will place heavy strains on the Government's resources of managerial, administrative and technical skills. The ability of the administrative machine to expand fast enough to meet the demands imposed upon it may, in the last analysis, prove the limiting factor in the implementation of the Plan."[11]

Sometimes plans contain evaluations of previous efforts that, while carefully avoiding open self-criticism, clearly attribute shortfalls to lack of adequate administration. Thus, Pakistan's second Five Year Plan partially explains the failure to achieve the first Plan's goals using such expressions as "nonobservance of the discipline of the plan" and "lack of vigorous efforts demanded for its implementation." Such references clearly apply to the government as well as the private sector. Paul Appleby's two reports on India indicate a widespread recognition of the importance of public administration. Even here, where according to Appleby, government is "highly advanced," administration must be constantly improved.[12] The conclusion is that adequate governmental capacity for decision-making and other activities required by economic growth is both essential and limiting.

One further observation seems called for at this point. New and inexperienced governments seem fated to undertake too much in the field of economic activities. They seem impelled to assume increasing responsibility either by inner compulsion or outside pressures. To characterize their activities as "too extensive" involves a value judgment, but the extreme complexity, number, and scope of the economic decisions forced on or accepted by most governments of underdeveloped countries makes the excess apparent to nearly all except those advocating centrally directed economies. The level of efficiency in many of these administrative activities is so low that even the imperfect markets in most of these countries could allocate and control resources more efficiently. In this ever increasing role of government lies one of the greatest obstacles to successful modernization.[13]

Governmental involvement in the economic activities of the community can be considered as forming a continuum ranging from "most" to "least." The "most" involvement would be those governmental activities having the most direct bearing on individual economic transactions and therefore presumably requiring the "most" administrative work; the "least" governmental involvement would require the least administrative capacity. For purposes of presentation, this continuum can be divided into five categories whose limits are appropriately obscure.[14]

1. *Operations.* These include the numerous instances in which the government directly procures and manages the factors of production, as in building factories, roads, and other construction projects. It also includes the provision of services, such as government schools, hospitals, roads, communications, police, safety. Even the role of government in the military sector is logically included—a sector often so large that its economic effect is very important.

2. *Direct Control.* This category covers those governmental activities that directly permit or prohibit specific economic activities, i.e., permits to construct buildings or establish factories, licenses to engage in business, assignment of market stalls, permission to obtain a specific loan from a bank. The essence of this category is its specificity and directness.

3. *Indirect Control.* Here, government involvement loses its specificity and government establishes the rules and conditions under which production and distribution of goods and services are carried on. The rules and conditions, though given for a group or type of economic activity rather than on a specific basis, are very closely and obviously related to the economic activity—for example, government control of the use of foreign exchange and of money and provision for commercial marketing arrangements, etc.

4. *Direct Influence.* The line between control and influence is hard to draw, yet important. It reflects the shift from coercion to advice and persuasion in economic activity. This category would include non-forceful attempts to persuade farmers to join cooperatives or to borrow money from government agricultural banks. It could include selecting candidates for overseas training programs or providing certificates of general credit-worthiness.

5. *Indirect Influence.* This is the residual claimant for government involvement in economic activities. It covers such important but allusive activities as explaining government policies to the people, setting examples of frugality and efficiency, and promoting a receptive attitude toward innovation.

There appears to be a marked bias toward the more direct or "most" end of the continuum, thus adding to the administrative burden. Characteristically, when the government of an underdeveloped country decides it must do something about an economic problem, first thoughts are apparently given to activities involving operations and direct control rather than to activities requiring less administrative capacity.

While empirical studies to support this observation are not available, the prevalence of rationing schemes, import licensing, and permits may be considered as part of the available evidence. New governments seem to understand and have more confidence in rationing and direct licensing than in persuasion or inducement through rewards and penalties. For example, the rather common practice of licensing individual imports generally encourages open corruption and windfall profits. Such licensing requires a great deal more paper work than would auctioning of foreign exchange to the highest bidder. Yet the latter method is used only by a few countries, while import licensing continues as a widespread bottleneck to necessary imports and a severe drain on administrative capacity in most underdeveloped countries.

There probably are many reasons for this bias. Market forces of indirect pressure through rewards and penalties may minimize administrative requirements, but such forces are often too impersonal to suit the political climate. Thus, the purpose of rewarding particular racial or national groups or political supporters may well conflict with administrative efficiency.

If there does exist a bias toward the "most" side of the continuum, it may result from a lack of administrative sophistication or the absence of appropriate institutions to make effective use of less direct methods. Here experience and economic growth may provide some improvement, though governments, having tasted the heady feeling of direct power, are usually reluctant to accept methods that seem to reduce their importance.

Economic Concepts in Development Administration

Since most administrators spend a substantial portion of their time involved in economic affairs, they must be given the opportunity to slough off some of the myths about economic growth that have accumulated in colonial folklore. They must be persuaded to be more effective in identifying and encouraging the tendencies that help growth and in reducing the innumerable barriers to growth. They need not be trained as professional economists, but in order to enhance the contribution of public administration to modernization, they must be exposed to some basic economic principles and tools.

Production and Productivity

Nowhere is there greater need for understanding than in the area of production and productivity. The general economic objective of the modernization process is to raise total and per capita production in order to achieve tolerable levels of consumption. This increase in production must be associated with achieving a capacity for self-generated and sustained economic growth to take care of increased population and further increases in consumption.

These are relative, not absolute, goals; they emphasize improvement, not a particular level. Persistent visible growth, even from low levels, is a highly satisfactory condition for a society to achieve. Even such modest increases in per capita consumption as 1 per cent to 2 per cent a year will, in a few decades, bring startling transformations in a society. It is the fact of sustained growth, not the amount, that is important.

Production is the utilization of the input factors of land, labor, and capital in the creation of the goods and services that a society wants. Production totals can be increased by applying more inputs and by increasing the efficiency with which the inputs are utilized in the production process. The method by which the input factors are combined is technology, and the optimum level of technology is that which makes the best (most efficient, most productive) use of available inputs. Increasing productivity is therefore increasing efficiency in the combination of inputs. Herein lies the essence of economic growth. Somehow, not only must there be more units, but the available inputs must be used more efficiently for greater output per unit of input.

The administrator in an underdeveloped country would profit greatly from a better understanding of the function of capital as an input in production. Too often the role of fixed capital, such as buildings or machines, etc., is so overestimated that capital is wasted. Further, productivity is assumed to be a linear function of capital; twice as much capital means twice as much productivity. It seems to follow, incorrectly, that the major "missing component" in the underdeveloped country is a stock of fixed capital. Therefore, all effort must be concentrated on accumulating fixed capital. Since most kinds of fixed capital are imported, the problem of development focuses down to buying or borrowing or receiving capital as a gift from abroad. Responsibility in the modernization process is thus shifted to the foreigner who determines the rate of economic development by deciding how many and what resources he will loan or give to the underdeveloped country.

At the other extreme is the view that increasing fixed capital is only of minor importance and that management and labor "know-how" is the only input factor requiring sharp expansion to achieve a significant productivity increase. This approach is most often applied to the agricultural sector where modern agricultural machinery has often been introduced before the recipients either need or know how to use it. The concentration on "know-how" rather than fixed capital is particularly pleasing to legislators of the advanced countries for obvious reasons.

Both of these extreme positions are substantially incorrect, but each contains enough truth to be perplexing. First, fixed capital is positively and functionally related to the level of technology though not in a simple, linear relationship. There are times when a great deal more fixed capital brings little more productivity, while at other times a little additional fixed capital can be associated with a very substantial increase in productivity.

Economists generally accept the thesis that the greatest increase in productivity comes from improved technology, not merely from increased inputs. This means that production, both total and per capita, will increase if capital input is increased, but the greatest share of the per capita increase will result from the improved level of technology generally associated with more capital input. It has been demonstrated with reasonably adequate statistical evidence over a period of about seventy years that, of each year's increase in per capita product in the United States, about one-tenth could be attributed to more capital input, and nine-tenths to improvement in the way the inputs were put together! Simply getting more capital will clearly not modernize the productive process if the added capital does not result in, or is not caused by, an improvement in the level of technology.

It is not necessary to assume a simple causality between fixed capital and the level of technology, but it is clear that an increase in fixed capital is directly related to improved technology. It is impossible in the real world to achieve a significant improvement in technology without an increase in the amount of fixed capital. In some very simplified operations, or in a narrow context, this direct relationship may not be evident. There may be countries where peasants increase productivity with their old equipment by changing their methods of planting. But efforts to introduce advanced techniques without added capital have often failed. Whether the added capital serves to make the new techniques workable, to induce the peasants to try the new methods, or even to reduce the peasants' risks in using such techniques, experience has shown that these innovations require additional capital, however varying in amounts and relationships.[15]

The average administrator must also learn to appreciate the role of the entrepreneurial function in the production process and in the adoption of improved technology. The capacity to make the kinds of decisions involved in the production process has been called the most critically scarce resource in underdeveloped countries. Absence of private entrepreneurial capacity is often given as the most important reason for direct government participation in the production process. Such substitution of one scarce input for another is not likely to lead to increased production.[16]

The areas of ignorance that surround the processes and institutions by which a society develops adequate entrepreneurial capacity are overwhelming. The process involves a wide and profound break with tradition and requires an understanding of the social role of the innovator as well as of the role of motivation in individual and social affairs. For example, the entrepreneurial function may be assiduously cultivated by a dissatisfied group or a class in society seeking to secure status or recognition through increased economic achievement.[17] Furthermore, the entrepreneurial function is usually not the same for government as for the private sector. The risks are different, the role of expectations is different, and the costs and benefits should be figured differently. This area of economic activity is almost an unexplored jungle, full of myths and traps, with only vague guidance from colonial experience or the traditional economics of the firm.

Public administrators are in a strategic position either to encourage or discourage the development of entrepreneurial capacity. Because government is so widely involved in controlling and influencing economic decisions, sympathetic government efforts can facilitate new entrants to production, new expansions of the market, arrangements for additional labor, and more flexible pricing practices. Breaks with tradition generally cause dispute, and administrators frequently become involved. A lack of governmental sympathy is a deadly burden to the innovating process.

Money and Prices

Money is a peculiar kind of social invention, ubiquitous and penetrating. It changes what it touches, and poets and philosophers have been filled with despair at its essential wickedness. Yet the modernization process of a society necessarily enhances the role of money, increasing its geographic spread as well as its influence. A good index of modernization is often the degree to which goods and services are produced for money rather than for barter or for home consumption. The widespread use of money makes possible the development of markets, of specialization, and of larger scale production. For good or for evil, the increased use of money is an essential ingredient in the modernization process; its misuse is often the basic cause of detours on the road to self-generated economic growth.

Government's relationship to money is obvious. Government

defines money, creates money, and prescribes the rules under which others can create and use money. While the average administrator does not become directly involved in formal monetary policy, there are many functional relationships between the government activities and the role of money in the development process.

One of the most important yet mysterious aspects of money is the recognition of the difference between a country's own money (domestic money) and the money of another country (foreign exchange). For although a country can create its own domestic money quite easily (in limitless amounts, if it can live with the consequences of such action), it cannot create foreign exchange. Underdeveloped countries undergoing modernization need relatively large amounts of foreign exchange, both for capital goods and consumption goods imports. Foreign exchange is generally involved in any significant economic activity, from the obvious instances in which imported machinery is needed to the less direct cases in which increased payments in domestic money increase incomes for workers seeking to buy imported consumption goods.

Government allocation of foreign exchange is therefore critically important. Nearly every government program and project either involves foreign exchange directly, or affects indirectly the demand and use of foreign exchange. Education programs demand foreign teachers and imported equipment and building materials. Factories require imported equipment, building materials, and, not infrequently, foreign managers and technicians. Road construction may require imported engineers and equipment. Even if only domestic money is spent for labor using only domestic capital equipment, increased income in domestic money means an increase in purchasing power and may therefore raise the demand for imported commodities. Any significant capital formation or improvement in technology is likely to require foreign exchange.[18] Furthermore, because foreign exchange requirements tend to go up as a society modernizes, the direction of its allocation becomes increasingly important.

Better understanding by administrators of the role of foreign exchange would lead to its more efficient use. For while foreign exchange seems inevitably involved in modernization programs and projects, the amount concerned and the returns from its expenditure may vary depending on specific administrative decisions. Over-purchasing of imported equipment for road projects is a frequent example of this variation. Similarly, the attitude of a whole community or section of a country toward the use of foreign exchange will often have a marked effect on the demand for foreign exchange. Here official example and explanation of the need for conserving foreign exchange may determine whether or not the community is responsive to government programs.

Scarcity of foreign exchange often creates curious pricing phenomena in underdeveloped countries. A higher priced article, made entirely or largely with domestic factors, may be "cheaper" than a lower cost article that must be imported. "Cheaper" in this usage obviously refers not to standards of formal monetary measurement but to broader differences between individual and social costs and benefits. While these differences are important in all societies, they are particularly important to developing countries where the divergences between individual and social costs seem larger and more strategic. The pricing machinery and marketing institutions, for example, are often too limited to relate market prices to social costs. When government activities directly affect entry into the market, the provision of raw materials, and the general availability and mobility of the factors of production, officials may make their most important contribution to raising production and productivity by considering the differences between individual and social costs and benefits.

There is an obvious, but often neglected, difference between the value of a good and the thing itself. Equally, there is a difference between financial and real savings, between financial investment and real capital formation. That an understanding of these differences is important to administrators becomes apparent when one considers government's role in encouraging savings and capital formation. An economically advanced society has developed many kinds of institutions and entrepreneurial capacities to relate the financial measurement of things and the things themselves. For example, personal financial savings in the form of life insurance premiums are accumulated by insurance companies and loaned to investors who order the construction of large office buildings. In most underdeveloped countries these institutional arrangements are nonexistent or very limited. The whole complicated process of diverting expenditures on consumption to expenditures that will result in fixed capital for future production is often assumed to occur spontaneously and without institutional requirements. The importance of this erroneous assumption is demonstrated in the numerous ineffective schemes for increasing savings. Fiscal institutional arrangements in the advanced countries took decades and even centuries to develop and evolved largely in the private sector. Development of institutions is neglected or attempted overnight by government fiat in many underdeveloped countries. Just as a farmer who saves enough domestic money to buy an imported implement cannot assume it is available, so a government official who secures a budget for a program must consider the institutional requirements necessary for transforming his financial resource authority into real goods and services.

Markets and Competition

The government and its administrators have a particularly important, if subtle, influence on the development of markets and the degree and type of competition essential in modernization. A society undergoing modernization requires that its marketing systems be extended and improved. Raising the level of technology, the major key to higher productivity, necessarily means greater specialization or more division of labor. Specialization is inconceivable without a more extended market system to absorb larger quantities of goods produced and offered for sale.

Effective marketing systems serve as mechanisms for developing and transmitting economic signals. These signals, usually in the form of price changes, indicate how the factors of production are to be utilized to meet the community's requirements.[19] Price increases usually encourage increased production while discouraging consumption, and price decreases usually have the opposite effect. Whole fields of economic analysis have been developed to explain, rather unsuccessfully, the functional relationships among these economic signals. These analyses are even less successful when applied to underdeveloped countries. Yet the development of improved economic signals and appropriate reactions to such signals is an essential of higher productivity. In underdeveloped countries it may be easy to exaggerate, but also easy to overlook this mechanism's importance in stimulating forces needed to achieve higher production and productivity.

Government plays a key role in all market systems. Even where government limits itself to establishing the rules, its activities are essential to efficient market operations. When, in addition, government participates actively in market transactions, controls or directs entry into the market, and allocates many of the scarce resources that affect reactions to economic signals, clearly the proper conduct of government is essential to expansion and improvement of the market mechanism.

Marketing systems apparently need some competition if they are to be effective. Here, too, economists have written whole libraries of books on how to measure the "some" and on the effects of limited competition on prices and reactions to price changes. Even with all the uncertainties and contradictions that make up our knowledge, some basic relationships remain widely accepted and are important in guiding official actions in underdeveloped countries.

First, expectations are basic to entrepreneurial reaction to market signals. As the level of technology rises, production tends to become more "roundabout," more indirect. The time span between the initial production decision and the final sale is extended. The need to predict the future enhances the importance of expectation in entrepreneurial decision-making. The modern production process is far more sensitive to government actions than production for home consumption or barter markets. When governments constantly change market conditions, they have a demoralizing effect on production decisions. Even when these government actions are internally consistent and in the right direction, they may affect expectations adversely. Constant "jerking" of the market signals may induce unfavorable expectations that will seriously affect entrepreneurial decisions on production and prices.

Second, production and marketing in traditional societies depend largely on limited entry and immobility of the factors of production. Expansion and improvement of markets require easier access and a greater ability and willingness to respond appropriately to market signals. Here, too, official action is strategic. It ranges from direct control of market entry, by licensing specific production activities, to influencing entrepreneurs and laborers to move to better markets. Competition often means breaking with tradition, as when the single village shoemaker is confronted with a new rival or with factory-made products. Sorting out the short-run and long-run benefits of these changes and evaluating differences between social and individual costs should take up a considerable portion of a subdistrict commissioner's time.

Third, the spread of marketing arrangements together with economic innovations, brings improvements in many other parts of the complex of modernization. For example, improved communications and greater political integration are key components in modernization. When marketing expands, bringing new producers and buyers, improved production techniques, greater entrepreneurial decision-making capacity, increased mobility of the factors of production, and more adequate response to market signals, it also fosters a new realization of what modernization means, more awareness of government, more contacts between groups and interests, and a greater diffusion of information about the nation.

It would not be difficult to add other illustrations to demonstrate the kinds of economic understanding needed by public administrators in underdeveloped countries. The problems of social and economic overhead investment, of external economies in production, and of improved income distribution, are only a few of the broad subjects in economic analysis that may be even more important than the illustrations cited above. Presenting these economic concepts in the technical terms of modern economics is inadequate. They must be related to conditions in individual underdeveloped countries which often differ markedly from the assumptions and premises underlying modern post-Keynesian economics. They must be explicitly fitted into the important role that government plays in the modernization process. Then they must be explained in a language that administrators can understand and relate to their operations in government.

Public administrators must understand economic growth in terms of governmental operations. The modernization process is far more than mere economic growth, though economic growth is probably the easiest element of the process to understand and manipulate. Economic growth occurs not just from economic activity, but from the interaction of political, social, and cultural changes that are inextricably interrelated in mutual causative fashion with economic changes.

Government performs an important function in the process of modernization, particularly in its economic activities. Government action often initiates economic innovations and improvements on which higher productivity must be based. Government is usually the major financial backer of the new investment that makes possible a higher level of technology. Government impact on economic activities is obviously powerful, and its effect on the main forces of development, for good or bad, is obvious. Under these conditions, efficiency of government operations becomes a major factor in the modernization process. Finally, a better understanding of the appropriate role of government officials in the economic activities of a country is of key importance.

NOTES

1. One only has to consider the extent and variety of current books on the development process to be impressed with the diversity of viewpoint and analytical approach. In a rapid survey Economics could be represented by E. D. Domar, *Essays on the Theory of Economic Growth* (Oxford: Oxford University Press, 1957); A. O. Hirshman, *The Strategy of Economic Development* (New Haven: Yale University Press, 1958); H. Leibenstein, *Economic Backwardness and Economic Growth* (New York: Wiley, 1957): Geography represented by N. S. Ginsberg, ed., *Essays on Geography and Economic Development* (Chicago: University of Chicago Press, 1960); D. Lee, *Climate and Economic Development in the Tropics* (New York: published for the Council on Foreign Relations by Harper, 1957); History represented by H. J. Muller, *The Uses of the Past* (New York: Oxford University Press, 1952); W. W. Rostow, *The Stages of Economic Growth* (Cambridge: Cambridge University Press, 1960): Political Science represented by G. A. Almond and J. S. Coleman, eds., *The Politics of Developing Areas* (Princeton, N.J.: Princeton University Press, 1960); R. A. Dahl and C. E. Lindblom, *Politics, Economics, and Welfare* (New

York: Harper, 1953): Psychology represented by Harold H. Anderson, ed., *Creativity and its Cultivation* (New York: Harpers, 1959); D. Mc-Clelland, *The Achieving Society* (New York: Van Nostrand, 1961); Sociology and Anthropology represented by B. F. Hoselitz, *Sociological Aspects of Economic Development* (Glencoe, Illinois: The Free Press, 1960); M. Mead, ed., *Cultural Patterns and Technological Change* (Paris: United Nations, 1953).

The following are also of interest: E. C. Banfield, *The Moral Basis of Backward Society* (Glencoe, Illinois: The Free Press, 1958); M. F. Millikan and D. Blackmer, eds., *The Emerging Nations* (Boston: Little, Brown, 1961).

2.   J. M. Van Der Kroef, "Economic Development in Indonesia: Some Cultural and Social Impediments," *Economic Development and Cultural Change*, January, 1956, p. 129.

For a good brief summary of the role of government in economic growth, both in the advanced countries and in underdeveloped countries, see E. S. Mason, *Economic Planning in Underdeveloped Countries* (New York: Fordham University Press, 1958).

3.   This latter point can be enlarged briefly to consider the curious and inconsistent attitudes toward government participation in the whole modernization process. The fallacious belief in a dichotomy between policy and administration is firmly held. The ordinary administrator is supposed to stay away from politics and political changes, concentrating entirely on implementing policies set by the "policy-makers" at the top. The attitude toward cultural change is clearly ambivalent. Since national culture deserves only pride, officials must strive to preserve and protect it. Yet, since cultural manifestations often visibly deter economic growth, here officials must both protect and change at the same time. Social changes, inextricably interwoven with political and cultural changes, are again usually considered outside the province of public administration. Psychological changes are also generally excluded, except for highly generalized axioms about inculcating habits of thrift, frugality, industriousness, and discipline.

4.   United Nations, Department of Economic Affairs, *Measures for the Economic Development of Underdeveloped Countries* (New York: Columbia University Press, 1951), chapters 3 and 4.

5.   See W. W. Rostow, *The Process of Economic Growth* (New York: Norton, 1952).

6.   John K. Galbraith, "A Positive Approach to Economic Aid," *Foreign Affairs* (April, 1961), XXXIX, No. 3.

7.   R. Lekachman ed., *National Policy for Economic Welfare at Home and Abroad* (New York: Doubleday, 1955), p. 81.

8.   Hirschman, *op. cit.*, p. 5.

9.   Pakistan, Planning Board, *The First Five Year Plan, 1955-1960*, pp. 83, 92.

10.   India, Planning Commission, *The First Five Year Plan* (New Delhi: 1952), p. 111.

11. Ceylon, National Planning Council, *The Ten Year Plan* (*1960-70*) (Colombo: Government Press, 1959).

12. Paul A. Appleby, *Public Administration in India—Report of a Survey* (Delhi: Manager of Publications, 1953) and *Re-examination of India's Administrative System with Special Reference to Administration of Government's Industrial and Commercial Enterprises* (New Delhi: Government of India, Cabinet Secretariat, Organization and Methods Division, 1956).

13. These observations apply to countries that include in their view of a desirable society the need for having a significant proportion of the production activities remain under private initiative and control. Where countries have made the decision to eliminate private enterprise, they have already opted for the most direct kind of governmental involvement in economic activities.

14. These categories have no merit other than that their small number and vague dimensions make it possible to cover the wide range of government activities in a brief, but comprehensive, fashion. Many common activities can appropriately be classified into several of these categories.

15. See Everett Hagen, "The Theory of Economic Development," *Economic Development and Cultural Change*, April, 1957.

16. See Hirshman, *op. cit.*

17. See Millikan and Blackmer, eds., *op. cit.*

18. It is true that the accumulation of consumers' goods as capital may not require the expenditure of foreign exchange, but it may have many foreign exchange implications particularly in regard to prices and the availability of goods for export.

19. As previously mentioned, this description is essentially limited to free economies, as distinct from a centrally administered economy. Yet even in the latter, the price system is used to transmit economic signals.

VII

Public Administration and the Private Sector in Economic Development

EVERETT E. HAGEN

THIS PAPER considers the economic aspects of the operations of private enterprise in relation to development, setting to one side the political implications of maximizing or minimizing the role of private enterprise.

THE NATURE OF THE DEVELOPMENT PROCESS

Development depends primarily on the efforts and resources of the economy which is developing. In recent years aid from Western countries, the Soviet bloc, and international agencies to underdeveloped countries amounted to about one-fourth of those countries' gross capital formation and less than 4 per cent of gross national product.[1] This fraction is not likely to increase markedly. Even if foreign sources should contribute all imported materials and components required for capital projects, yet all of the labor and many of the materials needed to construct them (comprising more than half the projects' total cost) and most of the energy and creativity needed to make them operate well after they are constructed, would in practice be indigenous. Roads or buildings can only be built where they are going to stand, and it is highly impractical to import huge crews of workers and their means of subsistence.

Large and impressive projects will inevitably constitute only a small part of total investment in economic development. For proper development, a country needs about a 4 per cent annual rate of increase in gross national product. The large projects typical of a centrally planned development program in a non-socialist country can contribute only a small part of that rate of increase. Indeed, any country that used the total resources available for capital formation for large planned projects would provide elaborate plants for a few workers while the majority enjoyed little improvement.

It is also important to dispel the layman's idea, sometimes unfortunately also embodied in economic theory, that increase in productive capacity results primarily from increase in the amount of capital per worker. The error is easily understood by considering United States experience. The amount of capital per worker has increased continuously in the United States. The process, however, involved not merely an increase in the amount of capital. The added equipment incorporated scientific and technical advances; it was used by increasingly well-educated and better-trained workers; the workers operated in industrial units in which organization improved from time to time; and no doubt various other factors operated to increase productivity as well.

For the period 1909-49, it has been estimated that if the only change had been increase in plant and equipment of types already known in 1909, the increase in output per manhour would have been not more than 25 per cent of what it actually was.[2] Other factors, therefore, especially the development of technical, scientific, and organizational knowledge, account for the bulk of increased labor productivity. Some such ratio is undoubtedly typical of other countries. Mere replacement of the existing amount of equipment with new equipment embodying technical advances, would bring a far more rapid rise in productivity than large-scale investment not embodying continually advancing techniques.

Finally, it should be noted that advanced methods, invented in the West, cannot simply be imitated or imported by under-developed countries without adaptation. The difficulty of introducing the spade in a country of barefoot workers who use the digging hoe illustrates the point beautifully. Pressing down repeatedly on the spade cuts the sole of a bare foot, even one toughened by years of walking without shoes. If this difficulty is remedied by placing a curved plate along the top edge of the blade, dirt packs against the plate and the spade does not release its load. Only when someone thought of running a round rod transversely through the handle a few inches up from the blade so that the foot might press on the rod instead of the blade, did the spade become reasonably efficient in a barefooted culture.

The efficiency of any enterprise or productive process in a

technically advanced country depends on a complex of relationships within the economy around the enterprise—supply of raw
materials and components; the availability of engineering, financial, accounting, legal, and other services; transportation, communication, power, and other facilities; economic, legal, political,
and social institutions; and values concerning interpersonal
relationships. Place the process or enterprise in an economy
without such auxiliary services, and, if it were run as it is in the
advanced country, it would promptly break down. To adapt it
to a different economy and society requires innovational acts
somewhat different from, but probably fully as creative as, those
required in the initial Industrial Revolution.

Creative human action is still a core characteristic of the
transition to economic growth.[3] Without creativity, capital formation would be largely wasted; fruitful private projects would not
appear in large numbers, and government projects would be
mismanaged, burdening the economy rather than furthering
economic growth.

GOVERNMENT AND THE PRIVATE SECTOR

What can public policy and its administration do to stimulate
private creativity as well as to further development directly? To
appreciate fully the important things it can do, we must first note
some exaggerations of government's possible role.

It is sometimes believed that if the proper framework for
public and private activity were constructed, human nature
would lead individuals to advance themselves and accomplish
economic growth. The concept that there is a generally right
framework—to cite extreme cases, that communism would
accelerate economic growth in the United States because it did so
in Russia, or that the American system of private enterprise would
be as effective in Russia as it has been in the United States—is
simply wrong. It overlooks differences in national character. To
cite slightly less extreme cases, the relationship in Japan between
government and private investment decisions, which is extremely
effective in inducing rapid growth in Japan, would probably
materially reduce our rate of economic growth if imported into
the United States; and so, conversely, would our institutions if
imported into Japan. There is no one right formula. In this

paper, I am discussing a society which is not violently against either public or private enterprise, so that there can be a fairly wide range of acceptable relationships.

Next, some economic theories must be considered. One theory argues that low-income economies must launch some large "social overhead capital" projects—large power plants, transportation systems, etc.—before development can begin. Private inability to gather together the capital needed for such projects is considered a crucial barrier. If sufficient capital could be mobilized through foreign economic aid or investment, or the fiscal power of the indigenous government, then the bottlenecks could be broken and growth would proceed. Social overhead projects are not nearly so fundamental as this argument assumes. Moreover, small projects in power, transportation, communication, and other fields can usually be effective initially. The path to development is not nearly so rigid as the argument assumes. However, the role of government should not be understated. Social overhead capital projects are often advantageous, and by constructing appropriate ones, government may often expedite growth.

Another economic argument is that growth is inhibited because the markets in low-income countries are too small to induce investment. To stimulate growth, the government must simultaneously develop all sectors of the economy so that the advance in each will provide added income to create a market for the products of the others. The fact is that in all but the smallest countries available markets are amply large to justify investment in improved processes in a considerable number of industries. Government planning of certain sorts is fundamentally important, but not the magic cure.

Finally, government operation of enterprises is thought to be desirable in some traditional societies because the spirit of entrepreneurship is largely lacking. At any given period the degree of individual innovational ability varies among societies. In some countries, even though the government provides facilities essential for economic growth and creates an institutional framework favorable to growth, no progressive private enterprises will appear, and economic growth will not occur without additional governmental action. In such circumstances, it is suggested, the government itself must plan and operate new types of business enterprise. In these conditions this policy is plausible. Some resources may be wasted, but the outcome can hardly be worse than complete inaction.

However, there are serious limits to the success of such a policy. If the individuals of a certain society are not enterprising, they are not apt suddenly to become so when appointed managers of government enterprises. Badly operated government enterprises will burden rather than aid progress. Where effective entrepreneurship is lacking, no policy for economic growth is apt to work well.

Turning from such lugubrious prospects, let us consider countries where many private individuals and government officials display some innovational spirit. What can the private sector in such a society contribute to economic development, and what can the government, recognizing the role of the private sector, do to facilitate development?

Individuals seeking to maximize profits, to enlarge their domains, to prove their capabilities, or to do whatever else is necessary to make private enterprise succeed, take advantage of opportunities for development. Their activity may range from increasing agricultural productivity, developing a steel rolling mill, an air line, or a coal mine, to improving taxicab service or substituting efficient retail stores for bazaars. Wherever they turn, their goal of increasing profit or expanding business will result in the allocation of resources to spots where increase in efficiency seems possible.

I suggest that resources are generally better allocated through this many-fingered probing for areas where one may profit by improving a process than by government regulation of manifold economic activities. The much-maligned profit system or the complex human motives which it symbolizes will often direct human effort into anti-social activity—monopoly, neglect of lower income groups, etc.—but it also channels human energies into areas where returns may be earned by providing economic services more efficiently. In other words, the profit system works toward an optimal allocation of resources. This allocation of resources into likely spots plus alert management, results in a diffused and generalized increase of output which is essential to a rapid rate of economic growth.

The efficiency of this probing activity depends partly on the nature of the framework or base provided by public policies. Consider how government action or lack of action may hamper the contribution of the private sector to growth.

First, administrative regulations are established to curb the evils of private enterprise. These, along with red tape and the bureaucratic tendency to dodge decision-making, may inhibit action in the private sector. But the prevention of a little possible evil action at the cost of much possible fruitful action is an expensive operation.

Second, the government may consume resources which could be put to more productive use in private investment. Government tax collections will reduce private expenditures.[4] Government expenditures of the tax revenues will then absorb labor and other resources. The least important government expenditures may be less beneficial to the members of the society than, for example, the private consumption plus investment which would be possible if government expenditures and taxes were reduced by one-fifth, or the private investment which would be possible if expenditures but not taxes were lowered and the surplus revenues were loaned to private investors. If government expenditures are high while taxes are not, taxes may not unduly reduce private expenditures, but government purchase of labor and other resources may make those resources scarce, raise their prices, and so deny them to private, would-be investors.

Third (and conversely), the government may keep the aggregate level of demand for resources too low. Take, for example, a situation in which the budget is balanced at a given level of taxes and expenditures, but private enterprises do not see enough attractive projects to justify purchase of available productive resources. Then by increasing its spending to encompass additional projects without increasing tax rates, the government may increase output, employment, and income. Or, if the government reduces taxes without reducing expenditures, taxpayers will have more income to spend, and their increased spending will lead to the same result. In addition to the direct benefit of a raised level of living, the enlarged market may stimulate additional private investment.

Fourth, the government may choose the objects of its expendi-

of the UN, the ICA, and the OAS, February, 1961, *Summary of a Report,* p. 14.

15. Jorge Franco Holguin, "Economic Policy and Planning," *New Economy Review* (Bogota, Colombia), June, 1961.

16. In their paper "Country Programming as a Guide to Development," *op. cit.,* Colm and Geiger give an extended account of the techniques used in pragmatic planning.

17. *Provisional Report* (Latin American Seminar on Planning), *op. cit.,* p. 8.

18. Jan Tinbergen, *The Design of Development* (Baltimore: The Johns Hopkins University Press, 1958), Chapter II.

19. Planners have generally and erroneously taken the view that the formulation of instruments for implementing plans is properly a "problem of political science."

20. The shortage cannot be eliminated completely, but this is precisely why it is important to make the most effective use of the available supply.

21. Ideally, planners should make every effort to leave project evaluation and the preparation of each sector program to the appropriate ministry or agency and concern themselves with project and sector programming only to the extent necessary to reconcile and rationalize competing sector demands with scarce resources.

22. *Provisional Report* (Latin American Seminar on Planning), *op. cit.,* pp. 4, 7.

23. Since some investing entities are likely to be unable to supply all the requested information, a certain amount of estimation based on indirect information would probably be required to fill gaps in the data.

24. A farm-to-market road might be essential to provide access to an adequate supply of milk for a processing plant nearly or already completed or a warehouse to store goods in transit might be necessary for a newly constructed port.

25. For example, a preliminary engineering survey to lay out a route for completing the Pan American Highway in Panama and Colombia is expected to take two years and up to $3 million to finish. *The Washington Evening Star,* March 22, 1962.

26. In particular, there is a great need for preinvestment studies in agriculture.

27. The number of hospitals without doctors and nurses and schools without teachers testifies to the fact that due account of capital investments is not always taken in current budgets.

28. John P. Lewis, "Notes on the Nurture of Country Planning," *Technical Digest Service* (Published by the U.S. Agency for International Development), II, No. 3 (January, 1962), 12.

29. *Ibid.*

30. Ahumada, Jorge, "Problems of Specialized Training Requirements as Viewed from Inside a Country in Process of Economic Development," in *Aspects of Training in Economic Development,* OECD, January 1962, p. 16.

31. See notes 8 and 9.

decision among them depend on the relative size of the competing purses. Government must decide among the interests of competing groups. To optimize economic activity the government must establish some major principles for the allocation of resources and set out a framework of rules for economic activity.[5]

To achieve ideal results is impossible. But what is possible is a sensible evaluation of priority for government and private projects and a sensible attempt to provide in time the governmental services needed to complement anticipated private or government activity. Such scrutiny is likely to produce far better results than complete failure to evaluate. If actualities differ from expectations, adjustments can be made.

The rise in GNP during the first Five Year Plan period in India and the first years of the second stimulated private investment much more than the government had anticipated. As the country entered the third year of the second Plan, foreign exchange was short because of unexpectedly large private expenditures for imports. The policy which would best meet the situation could not be chosen simply on the basis of general principles concerning the relative desirability of government and private activity. The government sought more foreign aid, tightened up somewhat on private foreign expenditures, and markedly reduced its own previously planned program. Students of Indian development agree that this course of adjustment was more advantageous than continued execution of governmental projects, all of which in an absolute sense seemed desirable.

Several factors work against the type of budgeting we have described. Every official resists yielding his prerogative to execute projects in his field of jurisdiction. There is a traditional failure to check on any senior official's execution of projects; in some cases, any over-all governmental evaluation is regarded as socialistic and undesirable. Whatever the cause, failure to budget in the ways indicated retards economic development.

On the basis of this rather negative discussion we may list some contributions to economic growth which government and hence public administration can make.

Government must provide the conventional public services efficiently, impartially, and in the volume needed by expanding sectors of the economy. It must expand and alter the nature of education. It must construct and operate many facilities for transportation, communication, power, and urban services, and must do so in anticipation of increased future need if growth is not to be hampered.

If saving in the country is too low to finance the capital formation required for an adequate rate of economic growth, the government must levy taxes in excess of its needs for its current services, and either carry out needed investment itself or lend the funds to private enterprises which can do so. Moreover, taking a broad view of its responsibilities, government must act to regulate the total level of spending in the economy. It is no longer appropriate for any government merely to conduct its own programs prudently and let the level and course of private economic activities take care of themselves. If demand is sluggish and some labor is unemployed or not fully employed, the government should spend or lend in excess of its revenues or use monetary or other measures to stimulate private activity. If private spending is high and inflation is occurring even though the government budget is balanced, the government must either reduce private spending by tax increases, banking controls, or other measures, or curtail its own expenditures, exercising the restraint necessary to hold them below its revenues.[6]

In these ways the government must serve as a balance wheel to maintain full employment. However, it must do more than this. It must create a budgeting system which will accomplish a number of new tasks. The benefit which will be yielded by the proposed projects of each public agency must be appraised in relation to the benefit anticipated from the projects of every other agency. The benefit from the least important government projects should be compared with the benefit or satisfaction from the private spending which may be possible if the public projects are foregone. Or, if additional public projects will be more beneficial than a portion of private spending, fiscal and monetary measures, or possibly other measures must be taken to curtail private spending and obtain resources for the government projects.

The complementary public services which any public or private project will require—transportation for a textile mill; training for new industrial workers—should be anticipated, and plans should be carried out soon enough so that the services will be ready when needed.

Decisions must be made concerning the activities to be left to private enterprise. Whether the scope left for private enterprise is large or small, government administration should be such that the impediments of bureaucratic delay and indecisions do not arise. And government enterprises must be so related to conventional government agencies, and so organized, that they are managed boldly, efficiently, and without petty bureaucratic delays.

The attainment of these contributions of government activity to economic growth depends less upon high policy than upon effective administration. The training of civil servants for these new tasks, the reorganization of public agencies and the relationships among them, and the establishment of procedures which will make the organizations function in new ways: these are the high duties of public administration when it faces the tasks of economic growth.

CRITICAL FACTORS AFFECTING THE RELATIONSHIP OF THE GOVERNMENT TO THE PRIVATE SECTOR

The counsel given above is of course a counsel of perfection. No governmental machinery in any underdeveloped country will perform these new functions perfectly. In many underdeveloped countries, they are performed very badly indeed. Four practices among many public administrators in underdeveloped countries are perhaps more crucial than others in hampering economic growth. I summarize these practices here in unqualified form. It should be noted that they are not all-pervasive in any country.

1. Bureaucrats are wary of granting any permission within regulatory discretion to a private enterprise. Tales of inability to obtain needed permits, franchises, or licenses simply because no administrator would act are numerous, well-documented, and startling.

Underlying this practice is a pervasive reluctance to exercise discretion. Subordinates at all levels refuse to take initiative or make decisions; everything is pushed up to the very top for decisions. This tendency is accentuated when the decision would permit action by a private enterprise. Officials often feel a general distrust of private enterprise; they regard profit-seeking as evil. It seems to them that what is to private advantage must be to the public harm. They fail to understand that the result, rather than merely the purpose, of private action is important in evaluating its desirability; that many activities are advantageous even though they may incidentally increase the profits of already well-to-do individuals. (This attitude is present in some degree even in technically advanced countries, but it is not nearly so widespread or deeply held there.) I am not referring to a conscious judgment that certain activities of the private sector are socially undesirable. Where the by-products of the pursuit of profit are harmful, an administrator may reasonably recommend new fiscal or monetary restraints, new licensing, or regulatory policies for certain classes of business establishments. What leads to harmful official action or lack of action is the deep-rooted, unconscious suspicion that private enterprise in general threatens the public welfare.

2. Budget practices inherited from colonial days often persist. Colonial governments performed largely caretaker and welfare functions, and the prime duty of the budgeting officers was to see that waste in the small things was prevented—that three clerks were not authorized when two would do, or more pencils ordered than were needed. When a vigorous expansion of governmental activity is desirable, such concerns may bind that expansion in snarls of red tape and slow it to a crawl. One crippling aspect of these old practices in some countries is that approval by a budget official must be obtained for each separate expenditure needed to carry out a project, even after the project has been authorized by the parliament and the funds appropriated.

3. Even more serious is frequent failure to construct any mechanism for coordinated evaluation of government expenditures. No informed choice is made among proposed projects or between government and private projects. One ministry or agency does not take the actions necessary to complement those of another. The economic impact of the total volume of government expenditure is not appraised. Fiscal and monetary policies

and the regulation of foreign exchange expenditures have no firm basis.

No mechanism is established for supervising the execution of projects adopted, or even for reporting on whether they are going forward. "The word is the deed" concept prevails; once a decision to carry out a project has been adopted, the deed is regarded as done. Underlying these practices is the feeling of many a senior official that budget office questioning of his projects insults him and his office and is demeaning, and the feeling that to check on whether an official is executing policies for which he is responsible is an affront.

4. A practice often harmful to growth is action to protect employment rather than foster growth. I do not refer to programs to create employment in countries in which there are many unemployed or underemployed workers. Rather, I refer to general opposition to projects that reduce the human and material resources needed to produce a given volume of output or provide a new and more satisfying product with a given volume of resources.

This practice results partly from failure to understand the process of economic growth. Economic growth proceeds by the continuing creation of technological unemployment. When the workers and materials rendered superfluous by technical advance are put to work producing other goods and services, aggregate production in the country rises, and the level of living can rise with it.

This concept is rather abstract, and is apt to run into contrary lay preconceptions in any country, underdeveloped or advanced. Other harmful practices, however, are certainly not mainly attributable to lack of education, training, or intellectual understanding. They arise from certain deep-seated attitudes which, to use a physiological figure of speech, rest in the gut muscles rather than in the brain. The roots of such attitudes are unconscious and can be understood only by a study of the nature of human personality and the processes of personality formation.

Omitting certain qualifications and complexities, let me suggest that the adult's fear of private business stems from arbitrary elements in the behavior of parents or other important elders when he was a child. Such arbitrary or authoritarian behavior usually stems from the parents' preoccupation with circumstances in their society which make them anxious, or from their conception of the proper way to raise a child, or, more commonly, from both. The children feels anxiety and fear, and, since he perceives that his parents love him and would not harm him, he is also bewildered. There is bred into him a sense that there are undefined threatening forces in the world around him. The greater certain tensions in the society are, the more likely it is that such elements will be built into personality.

Later in life, as this sense of the presence of undefined, threatening exterior forces continues, the individual will unconsciously seek some rationalization of it. Such fear, in the personality of many Americans, probably was an important factor in the hysteria after World War II that Senator Joseph McCarthy drew upon. Similar elements in personality probably also explain the unreasoning fear of government which renders quite a few American businessmen less than fully logical in their analysis of public policies. In underdeveloped countries, in which the conspicuous alien factors of the past were colonial control and large foreign private enterprises, private business comes to be a symbol of the undefined threat.

Another of the deep-seated attitudes that affects official behavior in underdeveloped countries is the sense of the great importance of authority and elite status. For centuries position and standing in such countries has depended not as much upon individual achievement as on the status to which one was born. Government officials, army officers, and the professional classes were automatically drawn from the controlling families of the society. To justify to themselves their privileged places in the society, elite individuals had to believe themselves superior in essence to the common folk. One external sign of their worth was their authority. From infancy every child in such societies senses the importance of status and possession of authority; he senses it in the relationship of his elders to each other, in their attitudes, in the tones of their voices. By the time he is an adult he clings unconsciously and compulsively to authority.

Centralized budgeting challenges the authority of officials to make final decisions concerning programs within their jurisdiction. Probably for this reason, officials feel that submission to budgeting decisions threatens their elite identity and is demeaning. The failure to establish mechanisms for checking on the execution of policies probably also stems from an aversion to impugning a fellow official's worth by questioning his actions.

The practice of passing all matters of judgment up to the top for decision no doubt also stems in part from this attitude toward the possession of authority. By making decisions, a junior encroaches on his superiors' rights to possess full authority; thereby he encroaches on their social position and questions their worth. In a sense, he presumes to be their equal. He shrinks from these consequences.

This practice, however, also has another cause. Facing a problem arouses one or both of two responses in an individual: it stimulates him by giving him a chance to test his ability; and it creates anxiety in him because of the possibility that he may fail. Which response predominates is largely determined by one's experiences as one grows up, especially by the reactions of one's superiors to one's explorations and use of initiative during the years of infancy and childhood. There is reason to believe that the anxiety response is more prevalent in underdeveloped societies than in technologically progressive ones, because of differences in childhood environment. Individuals who feel anxiety rather than pleasure when faced with the necessity of making decisions can relieve the anxiety by letting the problem be decided by authorities above them. When lesser officials do make decisions, they are apt to stress tradition or base their decisions on their authority in the matter, their right to decide, rather than on analysis of the problem.

Thus the forces which sometimes prevent optimum public administration and cloud the relationship between government and the private sector are unconscious personality forces. Even when individuals with such motives and values have seemingly understood the importance of new approaches and have adopted machinery for such changes, often the new mechanisms somehow fall into disuse or are subtly altered to become vehicles for previous practices. A humble recognition of how little can be done to modify the individual's attitudes should help us to evaluate more precisely the limits of influence that can be exerted and to be more effective in exerting it.

Where these conditions exist, how can they be ameliorated? How can public administrators who are advising the governments of underdeveloped countries help to bring the organization and practices of those governments into consonance with the requirements of economic growth?

The method generally suggested for altering practices and attitudes is advice and training. And, like most conventional wisdom, this suggestion contains truth. Officials being trained in public administration for economic growth should be taught the reasons for and importance of the modes of organization and the practices discussed above. They should be given the most imaginative possible exposure to the reasons for the superiority of some structures and methods over others. I need not expand on that obvious truth.

Administrators should also be introduced to economic theories of income and of value and distribution. The former body of theory demonstrates that under prescribed assumptions the private pursuit of maximum income leads to an allocation of resources which maximizes public welfare as well; and the latter shows that the operation of fiscal and monetary policy to assure optimum use of resources complements rather than interferes with price mechanisms. These intellectual structures of theory are intrinsically attractive, and, if imaginatively taught, they can lead some administrators to understand more clearly the impact of their policies and activities upon economic activity and the public welfare.

However, this does not end the responsibility of advisers. The process of change in public administration which must take place is not simply one of adaptation of traditional forms to new technological requirements. Rather, the procedures which are found effective in the advanced countries must themselves be adapted in part to the cultural norms of the underdeveloped societies. Every society as it develops will do things which reflect both the values and motivations of its members and their new purposes; each will be adapted to some extent to the other. The adviser must understand this. The adviser who simply tells officials of underdeveloped countries that they should copy the administrative structures and procedures of Western countries is no more imaginative than traditional officials who reject his suggestions.

The adviser should recognize that there is a reason for every human action; if policies which seem to him eminently in the interest of the host country are not adopted, he should try to understand the reason for their nonacceptance, and adapt his advice to it. If the importance of not giving up part of one's authority by delegating it is great, the adviser should try to devise and recommend new institutional relationships which will break the bottleneck of concentrating authority without requiring formal delegation of authority. If decision-making creates anxiety, the adviser should try to devise practices which will minimize the anxiety yet permit action. Of course this will not be easy, and the result may seem something less than perfect efficiency. But the result may nevertheless be the maximum possible efficiency, for the attempt to introduce into a society practices that run counter to the values of the society may be even less successful.

To be imaginative enough to understand cultures different from one's own; to be creative enough to devise novel methods which accomplish new purposes while satisfying old values— this is the task which the public administrator must assume, if he presumes to advise the officials of low-income societies. Creativity is needed in giving advice no less than in economic growth.

NOTES

1. P. N. Rosenstein-Rodan, "International Aid for Underdeveloped Countries," *Review of Economics and Statistics*, XLIII (May, 1961), 107-38.

2. Robert M. Solow, "Technical Change and the Aggregate Production Function," *Review of Economics and Statistics*, XXXIX (August, 1957), 312-20. Solow estimated that the share of growth in output per manhour during this period due to increase in capital per worker was not more than 13 per cent. The method of estimation is a complex one. His article generated much professional discussion, indicating that Solow's estimate should be increased, but to not more than 25 per cent. See, e.g., Benton F. Massell, *Statistics*, XLIV (August, 1962), 330-32. Solow's technical error consists in having attributed wholly to technical progress the increase in output which is due to the interaction between additions to capital and technical progress.

3. For a somewhat more extended discussion of these characteristics of the transition to economic growth see E. E. Hagen, *On the Theory of*

Social Change (Homewood, Illinois: The Dorsey Press, 1962). Even if pure imitation of the methods of advanced economies were possible, it would be disadvantageous, since expending the available resources on elaborate equipment for a few deprives the many of any improvement whatsoever. The principle involved is that of equalization of marginal productivity at the margin. Thus the aggregate increase in productivity resulting from the purchase of two thousand wheelbarrows may be greater than that resulting from an equivalent expenditure for one large earth mover. Of course application of this principle requires that less capital-intensive methods shall be available. In some cases they are not, and the creativity necessary to devise them does not exist, or is directed into other channels either by traditionalism or by pursuit of a false god of maximum modernization.

4. Not by precisely the same amount, but by the same amount less any reduction in private saving that is caused by the taxation.

5. If it were socially desirable that every dollar should exercise as great an influence over economic activity as every other dollar—or what is approximately the same, that the existing distribution of income is optimum—then fewer governmental decisions would be called for. However, in all societies the values of groups with influence decree otherwise.

6. In some situations full employment may be impossible without inflation. In this case the government must decide which is the lesser of the two evils.

VIII

"Planning the Planning" Under the Alliance for Progress

ALBERT WATERSTON

1

"IT IS THE PURPOSE of the Alliance for Progress," says the Charter of Punte del Este, "to enlist the full energies of the peoples and governments of the American republics in a great cooperative effort to accelerate the economic and social development of the participating countries of Latin America, so that they may achieve maximum levels of well-being, with equal opportunities for all, in democratic societies adapted to their own needs and desires." In order to reach levels of income which, within a reasonable time, would assure self-sustaining development, the Charter sets as a goal for each Latin American country, a per capita rate of growth during the next ten years of not less than 2.5 per cent annually. Since population has been increasing in Latin America at an average annual rate of about 2.5 per cent, an annual average rate of increase in national income of about 5 per cent is necessary. Only three or four Latin American countries have been able to maintain these levels of growth in the last decade.

It has been estimated that these high rates of growth during the next decade will require no less than $100 billion in capital funds, of which at least $20 billion is to come from sources outside Latin America. Domestic resources are to be increased by tax reform and prices and market conditions for exports are to be improved through commodity stabilization agreements, reductions in trade barriers in importing countries and the establishment of a Latin American Common Market. Latin American countries, therefore, are expected to be able to contribute "fully 80 per cent of resources needed" for the Alliance for Progress.[1] The United States government has indicated that it expects to furnish $11 billion of the external assistance required; an additional $3 billion is expected to come from private American investors, $3 billion from public and private sources in other capital-exporting countries and $3 billion from international lending agencies.[2]

The proposed level of investment for the next decade must be several times the amount invested in Latin America since the end of World War II. External financial aid alone would be more than three times the amount of all economic assistance received by Latin America between 1946 and 1961 from the United States and international organizations, including the World Bank and its affiliates, the Inter-American Development Bank (IDB) and other sources.[3] If external aid is forthcoming on the scale projected, it is unlikely that Latin American development in the 1960's will suffer from a shortage of capital funds.

To make effective use of the greatly increased investment, the Charter of Punte del Este recommends that Latin American countries formulate long-term comprehensive development plans, shorter-term plans and ten-year goals for education and public health. The period to be covered by various countries' long-term plans will range from four to ten years. In recent discussions, the period mentioned for the shorter-term plans is two years.

The Charter also requests that participating Latin American countries create or strengthen machinery for long-term development programming, complete projects already underway, initiate projects for which basic studies have been made and start new studies, utilize idle capacity or resources, particularly under-employed manpower, and survey and assess natural resources. Finally, Latin American countries are to facilitate "the preparation and execution of long-term programs through measures designed (1) to train teachers, technicians, and specialists; (2) to provide accelerated training to workers and farmers; (3) to improve basic statistics; (4) to establish needed credit and marketing facilities; and (5) to improve services and administration."

2

It is palpably beyond the technical resources of most, if not all, Latin American countries, none of which has much experience in formulating and implementing comprehensive development plans, to carry out so formidable an array of tasks without outside technical assistance. The Charter indicates that the United States government, the Organization of American States (OAS), ECLA and the IDB will furnish, or contract for, technical assistance to help Latin American countries. A Latin American Development Planning Institute has been established by ECLA to train Latin American officials for planning activities, in organizing and improving agencies concerned with comprehensive and sectoral planning, and in helping prepare national development plans. As a part of its general policy of enlarging its technical assistance and training activities, the World Bank recently established a Development Advisory Service to provide a crops of expert talent to furnish economic and financial advice to governments of the Bank's less developed member countries, particularly in connection with the preparation and execution of development programs. The Organization for Economic Cooperation and Development (OECD) is considering the establishment of an Economic Development Center designed to train planners and to provide technical help. Finally, other countries which trade with Latin America, as well as the UN and its other specialized agencies, will undoubtedly continue to furnish technical assistance to Latin America.

Thus, while there promise to be many international and national agencies providing technical assistance to Latin America, there is likely to be a serious lack of trained and experienced economists, statisticians, engineers, agronomists, and other technicians and administrators needed for planning and implementation. The demand for qualified technicians, already great, will undoubtedly expand rapidly as augmented foreign assistance programs gain momentum during the much heralded "Decade of Development," to which both the United States and the United Nations have committed themselves.

On the supply side, there is little prospect of a rapid increase. Any program to train planners takes time. The Latin American Development Planning Institute expects in the next two or three years to increase the number of participants trained in its courses to eighty and hopefully one hundred per year. Even if these ambitious goals are realized, the average number of trained technicians which will become available from this important source will be small, especially in the first years of the Alliance program. Moreover, to reach its training and other goals, the Institute estimates that it will need about thirty "highly qualified experts."[4] More effective utilization of available technical assistance would undoubtedly diminish the need for additional technicians. In some countries, there are probably more than enough for the time being. For the region as a whole, nevertheless, there will not be enough experienced domestic and foreign technicians and administrators to carry out the tasks of the Alliance for Progress. The shortage becomes more serious if account is taken of the language problem.

3

In formulating a comprehensive national development program, planners endeavor to make realistic estimates of financial and other resources and, within the limits of these resources, to establish priorities for competing sectors and projects. Similarly, each Latin American country participating in the Alliance for Progress faces tasks which exceed the capacity of its available technical and administrative facilities. These countries would be well advised, as a first order of business, to evaluate realistically their technical and administrative capacities, to set priorities for each planning task and to determine the extent to which their scarce technical and administrative staff are to be assigned to each task to yield desired results. By "planning the planning" in this way, a government reduces the danger of putting too great a burden on its technicians and administrators or of so dispersing its efforts that it ends up doing too little.

Most persons familiar with the piecemeal approach to the development of backward economies involving individual, unrelated projects without a common perspective or unifying framework of economic policy cannot but welcome the current trend toward orderly programming of investment through long-range, comprehensive plans. There are still those who equate planning with socialism or with central control of the economy to the detriment of private enterprises, but these are "a dwindling band." Arthur Lewis' statement: "The truth is that we are all planners now"[5] may have been premature when first published in 1949, but it is accurate enough today.

Some accept the desirability of planning, but take strong issue with the commonly held belief that planning requires the preparation of comprehensive plans. Albert Hirschman, for example, has contended that "the elaboration of 'overall, integrated development programs' is not essential, and in fact might be harmful . . . 'Good planning' means simply to have studied and prepared thoroughly a given project, that is, to have ascertained whether it corresponds to a real need, whether proper engineering and market studies have been made, whether full financing has been assured so that it will not remain half-completed for years, and whether alternative ways of filling *the same need* have been explored and rejected for good reasons."[6] Hirschman also calls attention to the fact that "total, integrated economic planning could and often does co-exist quite amicably with, and may serve to cover up, unregenerated total improvisation in the actual undertaking and carrying out of investment projects."[7]

Hirschman's viewpoint is a salutary reminder that aggregative, long-term planning without soundly conceived projects to implement it is, at best, pointless and, at worst, misleading. His, however, is not the position held by most economists with experience in developing countries. The prevailing position is that there is no irreconcilable gap between those who believe in the necessity of long-term aggregative plans and those who would limit planning activity solely to the appraisal of individual projects. These two points of view may be described as *macro* and *micro* approaches or, alternatively, as planning[8] and implementation.[9] It is a mistake to think of choice between these approaches because both are necessary.[10]

4

While this resolution of the issue may be theoretically acceptable, it furnishes little operational guidance to Latin American countries which seek to "plan their planning." The question still remains: what proportion of a country's available technical and administrative resources should be allocated to *macro*, or aggregate planning, and what proportion to *micro*, or implementation? There is obviously no one answer to this question. Mexico, for example, with considerable experience in preparing and executing projects and sector programs, has built up a statistical basis for planning and a trained and experienced cadre of technicians and administrators and has reached a stage of development in which substantial technical resources could profitably be allocated to aggregative planning without interfering with, and in all likelihood stimulating, its rate of development. However, most Latin American countries do not have sufficient experience, basic data, or technical and administrative staff to embark on full-scale, aggregative planning or even on the preparation of the projects needed to implement aggregative planning.

While most Latin American governments have some kind of central planning unit and quite a few have comprehensive development plans or public investment programs, practically none has enough well-prepared, high-priority investment projects ready to absorb the capital funds which are already available. Indeed, as the discussions of the Latin American Seminar on Planning, organized jointly by the OAS, ECLA, and the IDB, pointed up: "The shortage of specific investment projects worked out in full detail partly accounted for the fact that the principles of the Alliance for Progress had not yet been applied as generally, or as intensively, as might have been wished."[11] Of even greater significance for the future of the Alliance, is the fact that few governments possess the administrative organization and technical staff required to prepare new projects at a sufficiently rapid rate to utilize the large investment funds expected to become available in the next decade.

This is hardly surprising in view of the shortcomings of administrative organization and technical civil service in most underdeveloped countries. An aggregative, long-term plan can be, and often is, completed in such countries by a few technicians, especially when assisted by foreign experts, without much recourse to the governmental machinery. But it is usually impossible for a government to prepare and carry out numerous projects without heavy reliance on its administrative apparatus. The government often obtains foreign technicians and contractors to help, but because of the character, volume, and continuing nature of project preparation and execution, great reliance must, and should, be placed on the government services.

Since administrative reforms to improve project programming present many difficulties and generally take a long time to carry out, orderly preparation, execution, and operation of projects is more difficult and time-consuming than the preparation of an aggregative development plan. This does not imply that the preparation of a sound development plan is easy. It does mean that while the technical aspects of planning often present knotty economic problems, the programming, organizational, and procedural aspects of preparing and carrying out projects to implement over-all development plans present serious problems not only in economics, but also in psychology, sociology, and public administration.

Perhaps because of this, national planners, who for the most part have been trained as economists, have been most concerned with the perfection of techniques for determining the character and extent of resources available or necessary for economic development and with the allocation of such resources in the planning period to specific uses. They have been much less concerned with the administrative systems for carrying out development plans and programs. Consequently, the techniques for aggregative planning, imperfect though they are, have been more developed than the techniques for implementing plans. Prime Minister Nehru who, as Chairman of the Indian Planning Commission, has manifested a broad grasp of planning problems, has pointed out: "We in the Planning Commission and others concerned have grown more experienced and more expert in planning. But the real question is not planning, but implementing the Plan. That is the real question before the country. I fear we are not quite so expert at implementation as at planning . . ."[12]

There is a lesson to be learned in the fact that for India, after many years of experience with both planning and implementation, "the real question is not planning, but implementation . . ." The weight of India's, as well as of most other countries' experience, clearly indicates that if projects required to implement plans are to be ready and executed on schedule, many more technicians must be assigned to implementation than to planning.

There is a danger today that the enthusiasm for aggregative planning in Latin America may obscure the even greater needs of implementation. Unless adequate account is taken of these needs, others may find themselves in the unenviable position of the planners, who, after about a year and a half's work preparing Bolivia's Ten Year Development Plan for 1962-71 (which hopefully envisages annual increases of 8.3 per cent in gross national product and 9.15 per cent in the first five years), found it necessary to write: "The principal deficiency that will be noted in the formulation of the present Plan is the small number of specific investment projects, studied in all their details, which have been included [in the Plan]. It is a most urgent task that the pre-investment studies whose economic justification is given at length in the different sections of the Plan are now completed, including the pertinent engineering studies, so that their execution may now proceed with the speed that the imperative conditions require."[13]

5

"Planning the planning" for a country to achieve the proper balance between planning and implementation requires consideration of the *kind* of planning and the *kind* of implementation suitable to the country at its stage of development. Thus, a choice must be made between econometric and empirical or pragmatic planning. For econometric planning, a wide variety of mathematical techniques is now available. Under appropriate circumstances and in the hands of trained econometricians, mathematical growth models, input-output tables, linear programming, and the theory of games can make useful contributions to the internal consistency of comprehensive development plans. But in view of the gaps in basic statistical data, the inadequate training of most planners in Latin America, as well as the shortage of qualified foreign planning technicians, it is questionable whether advanced mathematical techniques can yield meaningful results in a reasonable period at the present time in most of Latin America.

Although nearly all Latin American governments now have central planning units, many are little more than paper organizations; frequently, they are out of touch with, and ignored by, the heads of ministries, official agencies and even the chief executives; they are always undermanned and their staff underpaid and undertrained. Although aggregative planning is gaining new status, at least as a means of obtaining foreign financial assistance, "it is still looked upon with deep suspicion in a number of [Latin American] countries . . . In addition to such mistrust, planning has been consistently fought by established political and administrative interests; as a result it has in many cases been entrusted to units functioning outside of the regular executive establishments. Such semi-autonomous bodies enjoy little communication with, and influence over the intrenched executive and administrative agencies . . ."[14] Even when not suspicious or hostile, officials commonly misunderstand the purpose and role of comprehensive planning. Thus, the former director of the Colombian Planning Department complained that, "I was constantly surprised during my two years as head of the Planning Department at the number of highly cultivated people who asked me the same question: 'Just what is planning?' "[15]

6

In view of the shortage of basic quantitative data and qualified technicians, the need to relocate, reorganize and gradually increase and improve the quality of central planning staffs and to teach government officials the meaning and purpose of planning, there is much to be said for beginning activities in most, if not all, Latin American countries, with pragmatic techniques which are easier to apply and understand than more sophisticated, esoteric econometric formulations.[16] The objectives of a pragmatically prepared plan should be limited, clear and consistent, and its targets should be few and realizable. It is not difficult to identify the critical sectors for Latin American development: for most countries, they are transportation, electric power, agriculture, education, and public health. A first approximation and a sensible division of available financial and real resources among these and other sectors is possible without abstruse and time-consuming mathematical calculations. The pragmatic approach accepts the fact that planning will be less detailed in sectors which are adjudged to be less important, at least for

a time, than in others which are consdered more significant for
the achievement of current objectives. Even in the most important sectors, pragmatic planning calls for planning inputs
and outputs of the minimum number of strategic factors needed
to affect other factors sufficiently to realize planning targets.

All available quantitative information should be used, and it
is "often possible to find officials, experts and other personnel
who are sufficiently well acquainted with their country, its
problems, and relevant aspects of such problems to be able to
make an extremely accurate contribution to an analysis of the
situation."[17] It is not essential to use input-output tables but
it is important that the input-output *approach* be used.[18] But
for this, a few conversations with knowledgeable technicians
should suffice in most Latin American countries.

While the instruments of policy for implementing the plan
should be even more detailed than for aggregative plans,[19] they
should not be based, as they frequently are, on the unrealistic
assumption that substantial improvements in public administration, taxation, and agrarian conditions can be achieved in two
or three years. Radical changes in these fields must be made
during the Alliance period if the program is to succeed, but
good planning requires a proper skepticism about the speed
with which reforms are possible in the first few years. A prudent
evaluation of possible changes is essential if realistic estimates
are to be made of the cost of achieving planning targets under
prevailing administrative, technical, and political conditions.
Failure to appreciate fully the high cost of inefficient organization and administration and the time required to eliminate ineffi-
ciencies is the principal reason for the underestimation of the
cost of achieving targets which is a well-nigh universal characteristic of development plans.

A pragmatically prepared plan should take far less time to
complete than a mathematically integrated plan. Colombia's
ten-year plan took two years to complete and Chile's, three
years; but it should be possible to prepare a pragmatic plan
for any Latin American country in no more than six months.
There would probably be many gaps and imperfections in this
kind of plan. However, since planning is a continuous process
anyway, and even the best plan usually needs revision by the

time it is published, refinement could begin immediately after the plan's completion. Meanwhile, the country would have, in a short time, an improved frame of reference for its investment decisions.

It will not be easy, of course, to find enough planners to complete pragmatic plans for each Latin American country in six months; but considerably less planners would be needed than for conventional econometric plans. Much more can also be done to simplify and rationalize planning, thereby further reducing the need for planners.[20] Most central planning units, for example, spend much time on the preparation, appraisal and inspection of projects and on setting priorities for projects within a sector. This is generally justified on the ground that ministries and other government agencies are not equipped to do the work well. If, however, most of the available technicians were allocated to this work in the ministries and official agencies, the central planners could give most of their time to planning and leave the preparation of projects and sector programs to others.[21]

7

A ten-year plan has the psychological advantage of targets often impressively higher than those for shorter-term plans. This advantage can be overrated, however, since the further away the target date, the easier it is for governments to postpone facing the unpleasant realities which must be met in the early plan period to make the targets realities later. Moreover, since investment activities for the second five years of the plan period obviously depend on unforeseeable international and domestic events as well as on accomplishments in the first five years, projections necessarily become vaguer until, in the last few years, they are usually little more than aspirations.

The longer the term of the plan, the less the degree of precision possible. As a practical matter, the period of the plan should be short enough to permit reasonably accurate projections and estimates and long enough to cover the gestation period of a sufficient number of related projects which give a reasonably adequate indication of the over-all effect of investment decisions in carrying out planning objectives. There is no hard and fast rule, but experience shows that a period of about four, or in some cases five, years meets these criteria. Colombia, even though it had a ten-year plan, preferred to replace it with a four-year plan which it is using as the basis for its investment decisions. Venezuela is also working on a four-year plan.

The adoption of a four-year period for planning would not, of course, prevent the setting of ten-year goals for education, public health, and other sectors as suggested in the Charter of Punte del Este. In fact, for agriculture, it might even be desirable to make "perspective" projections for fifteen or even twenty years. Only the combination of the various sectoral projections would be limited to four-year periods. The concept of a rolling plan, which has recently received increasing approval from planners, might usefully be employed with four-year plans. A rolling plan is revised at the end of each year, when estimates for another year are added. In effect, the life of the plan is renewed at the end of each year.

Frequently, development plans are not phased to show what needs to be done each year, especially in the first year. It would also be desirable, therefore, to prepare a one-year operational plan for the first year which would detail exactly what must be done to convert the four-year plan into a program of action. At the end of each year, a new annual plan should be issued as an operational plan for the next.

In its Santiago meetings in February 1962, the Latin American Seminar on Planning gave special consideration to short-term planning. It was the "unanimous opinion of the participants [that] the problems of planning in the short-term cannot be approached without reference to the more general and basic problems of long-range planning. In fact, it was suggested that, properly speaking, programmes should be referred to, not as short-term programmes, but rather, as transitional or temporary programmes, or as the short-term aspects of long-range programmes, or as short-term measures to be taken with the framework of long-range programmes . . . The short-term plan would be the medium for putting into practice what were, in effect, the first steps in the execution of longer-term plans."[22]

When short-term plans are viewed in this way it is hard to comprehend why two-year plans are needed. On the one hand, the small increase in time required to prepare a four-year plan instead of a two-year plan *by the same techniques* makes the four-year plan indisputably preferable; on the other hand, to be operational a two-year plan must be placed into two annual plans. It could be that those who prefer the two-year plan may have considered long-term plans prepared by conventional mathematical techniques and short-term plans prepared pragmatically as the only feasible alternatives. As suggested in this paper, however, there is also the alternative of preparing pragmatic long-range plans in a short period of time. Perhaps the most succinctly stated argument in favor of this alternative was made by one of the Bolivian delegates to the Latin American Seminar on Planning: "What is needed," he said, "is not so much short-term plans as plans prepared in a short term."

8

A two-year or other short-term plan represents an attempt to start and accelerate manifestly urgently and justifiable projects. There is, however, a more practical and expeditious way of accomplishing this objective. The danger in most Latin American countries is not that governments are less aware than outside experts of high priority projects; it is rather that in seeking to promote development, governments often seek to advance more high priority projects, as well as many of lower priority, than available resources allow. As a result, progress on all projects is slowed. Progress is also impeded by disorganized competition in some countries among more or less autonomous public or semipublic agencies and local, state, and central governments for foreign exchange, local currency, and other scarce resources essential for carrying out investment projects and programs.

While aggregative planning is beginning in the central planning unit, and even before, it would therefore be desirable, when adequate information on public investment is lacking, for an "inventory" to be taken of all public investments already programmed or in process of execution. Information gathered by questionnaire from all official investment entities, when collected, combined, and analyzed would permit rationalization of public investment in process and a balancing of total public investment with available resources. The following types of information would be requested for each project: the name of its sponsor (e.g., the central government, state or municipality, regional or other public or semi-public agency, etc.), an estimate of the time needed to complete the project, those responsible for the actual work (e.g., public forces or private contractors or engineers, whether domestic or foreign, etc.), the estimated cost in local currency and foreign exchange divided into annual amounts required, the arrangements for financing the project, etc.[23]

If a comprehensive plan already exists, the investment inventory could help reconcile current public investment activities with the national development plan; even when a development plan is not contemplated, an inventory could provide the means for obtaining more efficient use of available resources in terms of actual and projected investment. Indeed, an inventory could be the basis for the preparation of a country's first national development program. India's first Five Year Plan, for example, was little more than a compilation of projects and programs already in progress. The results obtained through the rationalization of investments in an inventory might thus provide means for securing immediate financing for obviously sound projects and programs while a more comprehensive aggregative development plan was being prepared.

The completed inventory for a typical country would probably show that more investment was being contemplated than could be covered by available financial and other resources. Therefore, in order to bring aspiration and reality closer, priorities, at least for larger projects, would have to be established. In some cases funds may be earmarked by law for specific projects, work on some projects of low priority may be too far advanced to stop, or a new project might have to be started in order to make a previous project effective.[24] Such cases are exceptions, however. Application of general criteria—tests of economic and technical feasibility—the sponsors' administrative readiness to execute projects on the scale contemplated, the adequacy of engineering and other studies, the reliability of cost estimates, and the adequacy of the financial contributions by the sponsoring entity or beneficiaries of the project, etc., should permit substantial reductions in the number of projects. The arbitrariness with which judgments are made on the priority of projects which had survived these tests, as among sectors, in order to bring the total volume of investment down to the level of resources would depend, ultimately, on the priority assigned to each sector. If comprehensive planning has proceeded far enough, these priorities should be available as guides; otherwise, sector priorities would have to be determined empirically on the basis of the available information.

From the review and evaluation of the inventory there should emerge a pattern of investment phased over time which provides for elimination of bottlenecks and maximum use of available resources. Greatest attention should be given to investments for the first year, which of course will necessarily require assumptions about investments in future years. Projects which are to be carried out in the first year may require the commitment of resources in later years, and projects which are to be started in the second or third year may require resources in the first year for preparatory work.[25] Inadequacy of information about natural resources and other basic data make it especially important that resource and sectoral surveys and feasibility studies be started as early as possible.[26] Where such sectoral surveys have been made, e.g., in Colombia, where power and transportation surveys have been completed, they have been of great assistance in preparing sound projects and coordinated sectoral investment programs.

When a development plan exists, the first-year program which has emerged from the review of the inventory should, of course, be integrated into the broader plan or plans. Where no development plan exists, however, the review of the inventory for the first year, when embodied in the annual budget, can become a one-year public investment program for the country. While such a program is more circumscribed than an aggregative development plan, it may still help rationalize public investment. In Mexico, for example, the Investment Commission, in the first two years of its existence, chose to prepare annual public investment programs in 1955 and again in 1956 in order to gain experience. Other countries have also preferred annual investment programs in the first few years of planning.

Whether or not the inventory of public investment is made a part of a development plan, it should be incorporated into a consolidated official budget which would include investments of the central government, public corporations, states and munici-palities, whether financed domestically or from abroad. Then, it is essential to systematic planning procedures that budgetary funds be made available only for projects and programs included in and for amounts prescribed by the public investment program. If capital and "capital-like" (e.g., education and health) expendi-tures are included in a general budget with current items, the effect of capital investments will more likely be adequately reflected in budgetary allocations for current expenditures.[27]

While the principles involved in taking a public investment inventory, rationalizing investment, and balancing public invest-ment with available resources are concepts which almost anyone can understand, few Latin American countries have enough trained personnel to carry out these tasks. It would be possible, of course, to import foreign technicians to take the inventory, review the data, and produce a good public investment program. This approach would have the advantage of speed, but at the sacrifice of an exceptional opportunity to use the inventory and its review for making more lasting improvements in the country's programming process.

When faced with the choice of getting quick results without lasting benefits or delaying results and making more permanent improvements in its programming procedures and institutions, Latin American countries would be wise to choose the latter. The first objective should not be quick results or even "the best decisions but a better decision-making process. . . . The produc-tion of . . . a good 'plan'—for the next one, five, or seven years seldom is as important as is even a modest gain in the rationality of the planning process, which will be authoring decisions for decades to come. . . . [For technical assistance purposes, this implies] that training is by all odds the most important function of any consultant group. . . . While the special classes and courses they conduct will be important, they must do even more of their teaching through day-to-day work with their indigenous counter-parts . . . through a work program in which their indigenous associates can effectively participate. . . . [Moreover], the con-sultants must work with the 'raw material' at hand."[28]

If this sensible advice were applied, most inventory and

programming work would be done by nationals of the country involved, with the foreign consultants playing the role of teachers and advisers, instead of doers. The consultants' success would be judged, as Lewis says, not by their erudition or even by the decisions they recommend, but "by the quality of the going . . . establishments"[29] they leave behind. If, moreover, the indigenous associates had the confidence of, and were responsible to, the ministers or heads of official agencies most concerned with public investment, and a conscious effort were made to set up the persons trained by the consultants as the nuclei of permanent programming units in the ministries and agencies, the transient results obtained from the inventory and its review could be extended to yield even more lasting benefits.

Some comment is in order about the professional prerequisites required of the indigenous associates. Sound programming of projects and the preparation of sector programs call for both technical and economic knowledge. Engineers (or other technicians) without economics or economists without technical information are equally inadequate for good programming. However, while economists generally make better planners than technicians, experience shows that engineers, agronomists, or other technicians who have acquired some competency in economics are more suitable than economists for project and sector programming. Dr. Jorge Ahumada, who has had considerable experience in programming for Latin American development and in conducting ECLA training courses, points out that "Actual programming work in Latin America has demonstrated that it is very difficult to become a good specialist in sectorial programming without a minimum technological knowledge of the field. . . . It is easier to train people possessing a technical background with some knowledge of economics to be good sectorial programmers than it is to provide economists with the minimum technical education necessary."[30]

Finally, there is the question of the official agency in each government best qualified to conduct the inventory and its review. The substance of an investment inventory and its review is the subject matter of implementation rather than planning.[31] Although the central planning organization has a legitimate interest in seeing to it that ministries and official agencies prepare and carry out investment programs which will lead to the realization of the targets in the plan, the prime responsibility for the preparation and execution of investment programs belongs to the operating ministries and agencies. In the ideal situation, therefore, each ministry and investing agency should carry out the inventory and review for the sector or portion of a sector under its jurisdiction. On the basis of an aggregative development plan prepared by a central planning body which allocates financial and other resources to each sector or portion of a sector, each ministry or agency would prune and shape its own investment program to make it conform to the requirements of the development plan devised by the central planning organization. However, since few operating ministries and agencies have the capacity to carry out these tasks unaided, some means must be found to assist them.

While it would be possible, at least in some countries, for the central planning body to supervise the conduct of the inventory and its review and to help establish programming units in the ministries and agencies, it would be unwise, in my view, to assign these tasks to that body. Central planning organizations in Latin America will have all they can do to establish and staff themselves and to formulate comprehensive development plans within reasonably short periods, to require them, in addition, to take prime responsibility for the inventory and its review and the establishment of project programming facilities in ministries and agencies, not only would reduce their capacity to prepare aggregative plans, but would also increase the risk, given present attitudes of operating ministries and agencies toward central planning bodies, that disagreements would arise which would impede the taking of the inventory and its review and postpone the establishment of programming units in ministries and official agencies.

In order to minimize these dangers while taking account of the legitimate interests of both central planning bodies and operating ministries (and agencies), it may be worthwhile to establish a training center in each country as an independent body, for the purpose of training technicians in the ministries and public agencies through on-the-job training courses to prepare sound projects and sector programs, set up project and sectoral progress reporting systems which would mesh with the progress reporting system of the central planning body for the comprehensive plan, improve administrative procedures and organization for project programming and execution, and prepare ministry and other personnel for proper operation and maintenance of completed projects.

The foreign consultants who were to act as advisers and supervise the conduct of the inventory and train personnel in the process, would report to the training center. However, the local technicians from the ministries would, although working on the inventory or participating in other training programs under the auspices of the training center, remain responsible to the appropriate officials (preferably the heads) of the ministries or agencies where they were employed. This administrative arrangement is desirable because (1) it would provide necessary assurance to ministers and agency heads that they will be involved through their own subordinates in the inventory and review, and (2) it would provide a convenient avenue of communication between the foreign consultants in the training center and the top officials of the ministries and agencies.

The staff of the training center in each country would be small and would largely consist of temporary international consultants whose sponsorship would be such as to engage the confidence of the central planning unit as well as the ministries and agencies. As a "third force," dedicated to the objectives of aggregative development planning but free of the ministerial suspicion or hostility with which most central planning organizations must now contend, it would be in a much stronger position than the central planning body gradually to bring programming practices in the operating agencies in line with the requirements for systematic aggregative planning. In the inevitable conflicts of view between the central planning organization and the ministries and agencies, a sympathetic training center, unaffiliated with either contender, could act as an "umpire" and use its good offices to reconcile differences. Eventually, the training center should work itself out of a job but at first it could prove the vehicle for relieving the central planning unit of ministerial programming activities which could easily, on the one hand, interfere with its urgent task of comprehensive planning, and on the other, arouse the suspicions of the ministries that the central planning body was seeking to meddle in operations.

10

In summary, the first planning job under the Alliance for Progress is neither to prepare long and short-term aggregative development plans for each Latin American country, nor to prepare projects and sector programs. Both are important, but the most immediate task is "planning the planning" of each country in order to assure that available technical and administrative facilities are realistically evaluated and distributed among planning and implementation activities. In all Latin American countries the needs for implementation will greatly exceed those for planning, although the ratio will differ from country to country. It has been suggested that, at least at the beginning of the Alliance period, pragmatically prepared plans are preferable to mathematically oriented ones. The greatest need is "not so much short-term plans as plans prepared in a short term."

As a first step toward rationalizing *current* public investment, an "inventory" of public investments should be taken in countries where information on the extent and composition of public investment is incomplete. The inventory should improve the existing public investment pattern. But more lasting results can be gained by training nationals in the investment decision-making process, and by establishing programming units in each of the ministries and public agencies to complement and cooperate with central planning organizations.

There can be no assurance, of course, that the prototype presented in this paper will work in any Latin American country. Clearly, the model would have to be adapted to each country's special needs. Moreover, many other prototypes might work as well or better. But this would only point up the need for "planning the planning" in each country.

NOTES

1. U.S. Secretary of the Treasury, Douglas Dillon, as quoted in the *New York Times,* December 1, 1961.

2. U.S. Secretary of the Treasury, Douglas Dillon, as quoted in Department of State, "Press Release No. 587," August 22, 1961, pp. 5-6.

3. Foreign economic assistance to Latin America from these sources totaled $6.3 billion. U.S. Senate, 87th Congress, 2nd Session, *Special Report on Latin America,* November and December 1961. Exhibits 3 and 4, pp. 47-48.

4. ECLA, *Noticias de la Cepal,* VII, No. 6 (January 26, 1962), pp. 4, 7.

5. W. A. Lewis, *The Principles of Economic Planning* (2d ed.; London: Dennis Dobson Ltd., 1954), p. 14.

6. Albert O. Hirschman, "Economics and Investment Planning: Reflections Based on Experience in Colombia," *Investment Criteria and Economic Growth* (Bombay: Asia Publishing House, 1961), pp. 38-39. Professor Hirschman wrote these words in 1954. He has since modified his position. See *The Strategy of Economic Development* (New Haven: Yale University Press, 1958), footnote 5, p. 78.

7. *Op. cit.,* p. 39.

8. Planning involves (a) an estimation of financial, manpower, and other real resources based on expected levels of income, consumption, savings, and investment (domestic and foreign), exports and imports, population and labor force, etc.; (b) the distribution of these resources on the basis of expected yields from investment (incremental capital-output ratios) among the various sectors of the economy in a manner calculated to achieve planning objectives and targets; (c) formulation of instruments of economic policy for realizing planning objectives and targets; (d) the reporting and evaluation of plan execution; and (e) at appropriate times during the planning period, recommending to the government courses of action necessary to achieve planning objectives.

9. As used in this paper, "implementation" includes the programming or preparation as well as the execution of projects, the programming and carrying out of feasibility studies, pre-investment and sectoral surveys, the preparation and execution of sector programs, and reporting on the progress of projects and sector programs.

10. Gerhard Colm and Theodore Geiger, "Country Programming as a Guide to Development," in *Development of the Emerging Countries* (Washington, D.C.: The Brookings Institution, 1962), p. 68.

11. Findings of the Latin American Seminar on Planning held in Santiago, Chile, February 19-24, 1962, *Provisional Report,* p. 6.

12. "Address by the Prime Minister of India to the Seventh Annual General Body Meeting of the Indian Institute of Public Administration," *The Indian Journal of Public Administration,* VII, No. 4 (October-December 1961), 435.

13. *The Economic and Social Plan 1962-1971,* printed in *Planeamiento* (official publication of the National Planning Office, La Paz, Bolivia), I, No. 3-4-5 (September, 1961), 33. (Quotation translated by the author.)

14. Technical Mission organized by the Inter-American Planning Society, with financial support from the Ford Foundation and cooperation

tures unwisely, or not draw the line between public and private expenditures wisely. Before a government decides upon the monetary or fiscal policies to affect the levels of aggregate demand, it must range its own development projects as well as anticipated private activity in some rough order of importance. It must compare the least important government projects with the least important private investment projects and compare both with the desirability of reducing or increasing the private income available for consumption. It can then choose a policy which will increase or decrease aggregate demand in the most advantageous way. In short, it must influence not merely the level but also the composition of aggregate demand. Only through such considerations can government avoid influencing the economy in an inadvertent and unconsidered way.

Moreover, it is important that government relate its proposed activities to anticipated private projects not merely by assigning priorities but by considering the technical relationships among its own projects and between its projects and private activity. If a desired project requires better educated workers, more power, or a new road or railroad, to achieve optimum results, government should either provide these facilities, or, if it seems more advantageous, allow private enterprise to do so for profit. Such planning of inter-industry relationships of course requires forward planning. The government is not being of maximum help if it begins to plan this year a power project which is needed this year; it should have done a projection five years ago and begun planning the project then, in time for its completion by this year.

Government limits private enterprise when it overregulates or when it refuses to make decisions under its regulations; and it limits private enterprise when it fails to do a good job of economic planning or budgeting which aims at an optimum level of aggregate demand and an optimum composition of aggregate output. I have suggested that private enterprises can usually decide the detailed allocation of resources among private activities better than government. This principle needs qualification, however. Different types of private activity, e.g., luxury hotel development and agricultural loans, meet the demands of different groups of individuals. It may not be desirable to let the